A Model for Work-Based Learning

WITHDRAWN

Belle Alderman
Patricia Milne

The Scarecrow Press, Inc.
Lanham, Maryland • To
2005

SCARECROW PRESS, INC.

Published in the United States of America
by Scarecrow Press, Inc.
A wholly owned subsidiary of
The Rowman & Littlefield Publishing Group, Inc.
4501 Forbes Boulevard, Suite 200, Lanham, Maryland 20706
www.scarecrowpress.com

PO Box 317
Oxford
OX2 9RU, UK

British Library Cataloguing in Publication Information Available

Library of Congress Cataloging-in-Publication Data

Alderman, Belle Y.
  A model for work-based learning / Belle Alderman, Patricia Milne.
    p. cm.
  Includes bibliographical references and index.
  ISBN 0-8108-5020-6 (pbk. : alk. paper)
  1. Education, Cooperative. 2. Experiential learning. 3. Mentoring in
education. I. Milne, Patricia, 1939– II. Title.

  LC1049.A53 2005
  371.227—dc22
                                                    2005010571

Contents

Tables and Figures

Tables

Figures

Preface

Work-based learning, where professional work experience is closely integrated with professional studies, now forms an important part of many courses in tertiary institutions. How such learning should be designed, implemented, and monitored to achieve quality learning outcomes is the subject of much debate.

This book offers a work-based learning model designed to enhance the experience through facilitated mentoring and reflective learning. The work-based learning model is based on an internship which has proved highly successful over the last ten years at the University of Canberra. In 1994, the authors developed a work-based learning internship for an undergraduate course in library and information studies. With the aid of a university grant, all aspects of the internship were documented, monitored, and evaluated. Its early success led to a second university grant and the production of a manual and accompanying video to enhance the preparation of students. At the completion of each cycle of the internship, further modifications and enhancements were made based on feedback from those involved. Three published articles in education and librarianship journals trace the evolution of the model, and discussions with colleagues during two conference presentations have enhanced its features.

We believe that the work-based learning model is applicable to other professional courses within tertiary environments, hence our development of this publication. We have extracted the successful features and provided practical advice on how to implement the work-based learning model. We have featured the aspects we believe to be the hallmarks of its success: a shared vision developed through training of mentors in the workplace and students, clear documentation, facilitated mentoring in the workplace, experiential learning theory enhanced by reflective strategies, and an emphasis throughout on student-centered learning.

The work-based learning model features collaborative teaching and learning where educators in the tertiary environment and mentors in the workplace work together. This collaboration produces work-based learning experiences designed around an individually tailored plan of learning. The work-based learning model uses the plan of learning to bring together theory and practice, thereby enhancing all university studies. Students experience the application of theory in a "real" situation and draw upon their learning experiences when discussing theory. The plan of learning provides the framework for student learning and facilitates linkages between the world of tertiary professional education, the world of work-based learning, and the world of student experience.

A Model for Work-Based Learning is aimed at all tertiary educators who are involved in the design and delivery of professional courses incorporating a work-based learning component. The generic nature of the model enables it to be easily adapted for a wide range of professional courses and for a diversity of organizational cultures.

Part I sets out the research base for all aspects of the model and shows how a program based on the theoretical model can be implemented. The model brings together facilitated mentoring as well as practices to support reflective learning based on experiential learning theory. Both of these facilitate links between three interrelated "worlds" of learning experienced by the student: the world of student experiences, the world of work-based learning, and the world of tertiary professional education. In chapter 1 these "worlds," and the links between them, are explored. A timeline for implementing the model is provided which will enable the reader to gain an overview of the practicalities involved in managing the program. Each phase of the program is then explained in some detail.

Chapter 2 examines the theory of experiential learning. It covers issues such as turning the experience into learning and creating a climate for reflective learning. This section also gives some examples for applying the theory.

Proven strategies for enhancing student learning are provided in chapter 3. These include strategies that encourage students to practice reflective learning, to use journals to assist them with this process, to provide evidence of their learning through the use of portfolios, and to develop skills of self-assessment. Other strategies that move the student beyond personal reflection are also examined. These include strategies to facilitate case-based and problem-based learning.

Ten years of experience in using this model has shown that where the student/workplace supervisor relationship is based on a facilitated mentoring model, enhanced learning outcomes are the result. Chapter 4 examines the concept of mentoring, its potential as a facilitating mechanism in work-based learning, and explains how it has been used in this model.

Evaluating learning is always a challenge in any educational process. Chapter 5 discusses strategies to monitor and evaluate students' achievements and those which ensure the model itself is effective.

Chapter 6 provides details to assist with the practical application of the model. It expands on the introductory overview provided in chapter 1, clearly indicates the roles and responsibilities of the key stakeholders, and describes the set of documents that is needed to support the program.

The conclusion, chapter 7, notes what the authors believe are the critical success factors of the work-based learning model. Also, drawing on anecdotal evidence from ten years of implementing and refining the model themselves, the authors confirm its value to students and mentors alike.

Part II contains a range of activities that can be used by educators during all aspects of the work experience, from preparing students and mentors through to assisting students to move into the professional workforce. It also includes examples of the documents used to support the model and referred to in part I.

Part I

1

Introduction:
Linking Worlds of Learning for
Enhanced Learning Outcomes

Experiential learning forms a significant component of the educational process in some disciplines, such as medicine. Others, including education and nursing, have recognized its value and include blocks of fieldwork. Students, educators, and employers alike often view experiential learning opportunities as ultimately producing more competent entry-level professionals.

Properly planned, designed, and monitored experiences expose students to the professional culture and workplace practices, ensure an easier transition from study to employment, as well as develop knowledge, skills, and attributes that are difficult to foster with academic studies alone. They bring together theory and practice, thereby enhancing all tertiary studies by allowing students to experience the application of theory in a "real" situation and by drawing upon the learning experience when discussing theory.

Those offering effective work-based learning experiences recognize that individual learning is developmental, requiring opportunities for practice, critical analysis, and reflective thinking. Best practice modeled by mentors (workplace supervisors) provides guidance and inspiration. Through work-based experience, students gain many opportunities for

- consolidating their knowledge of workplace practices and the professional culture
- thinking, reflecting, and evaluating theory and practice
- capitalizing on knowledge and skills they gain by linking coursework assessment and workplace practices

A collaborative teaching and learning model in which educators and mentors together provide learning experiences for students is presented. The collaboration produces work-based learning experiences as an integral part of professional courses. This activity in no way implies that the educator's responsibility is being abrogated; rather, it is recognizing that professional education alone, by its very nature, cannot provide the necessary range of educational experiences. Nor is tertiary education alone able to develop a concept of the profession or professionalism in the same way that can be gained from working alongside committed practitioners. But designing and providing quality learning experiences and ensuring positive outcomes can be difficult for the tertiary institution, the organization offering experiences, and the student.

At its core, the work-based learning model features facilitated mentoring and reflective practices based on experiential learning theory. These are designed to facilitate the links between three interrelated "worlds" of learning experienced by the student:

- the world of student experience which includes the knowledge, skills, and attitudes the student already possesses as well as their own personal perspectives, values, and fundamental understandings.

- the world of tertiary professional education, which includes the academic processes that have shaped, and continue to shape, the student. In the model, this world is represented by the educator.

- the world of the work-based learning experience which provides the physical context for the learning. A significant element of this world is the mentor who collaborates with the educator and the student to design a plan of learning and to facilitate the reflective learning processes.

The work-based learning model is represented in figure 1.1. The three worlds are linked by the relationships formed through interactions between educators, students, and mentors. These interactions are supported through the processes of facilitated mentoring and reflective learning practices which, in turn, influence and impact on the three worlds.

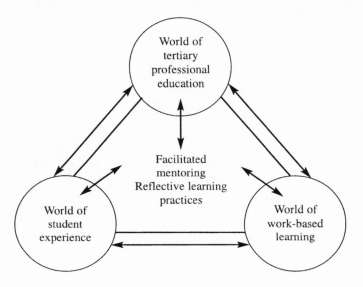

Figure 1.1   Work-Based Learning Model

There are a number of underlying principles and resulting actions.

- Learning builds on the individual's stage of development; *therefore, students must assess past and present achievements, identify goals, and set future directions.*

- Learning is a continuing process of creating knowledge; *therefore, students must continually reflect upon what and how they learn, how what they learn builds new knowledge, and how knowing how they learn affects future knowledge building.*

- Learning in the workplace is best positioned after the completion of core professional studies.

- Learning in the workplace can be effectively enhanced through a facilitated mentoring program.

- Learning is enhanced when theory and practice mutually reinforce one another.

- Learning is enhanced when individual learning, tertiary studies, and work-based experience are closely interlinked.

Overview of the Work-Based Learning Model

Table 1.1 Sequence of Activities in the Work-Based Learning Model

Ensure open communication | Continuing reflection

<table>
<tr><th colspan="2">EDUCATORS</th><th>STUDENTS</th><th>MENTORS</th></tr>
<tr><td colspan="4">Reflect, revise, and enhance whole process</td></tr>
<tr><td colspan="4">PREPARATION PHASE</td></tr>
<tr><td colspan="2">Gain support from professional community</td><td rowspan="2"></td><td rowspan="2"></td></tr>
<tr><td colspan="2">Develop support materials</td></tr>
<tr><td>Identify students and commence workshops</td><td>Identify mentors and match students and mentors</td><td>Attend workshops</td><td></td></tr>
<tr><td colspan="2" rowspan="3"></td><td>Develop resumés and send to mentor</td><td></td></tr>
<tr><td></td><td>Receive resumés from students</td></tr>
<tr><td colspan="2">Meet informally</td></tr>
<tr><td colspan="2" rowspan="2">Run workshop for mentors</td><td rowspan="2"></td><td>Attend workshop</td></tr>
<tr><td>Develop plan of learning</td></tr>
<tr><td colspan="2"></td><td colspan="2">Discuss plan of learning</td></tr>
<tr><td colspan="2">Approve plans of learning</td><td colspan="2"></td></tr>
</table>

<table>
<tr><td colspan="4">EXPERIENCE PHASE</td></tr>
<tr><td rowspan="2"></td><td rowspan="9">Write and reflect in journals

Develop portfolios</td><td colspan="2">Commence first block of work-based learning</td></tr>
<tr><td colspan="2" rowspan="2">Complete Charting Student Progress Guide</td></tr>
<tr><td rowspan="2">Visit students and mentors</td></tr>
<tr><td colspan="2">Talk with academics</td></tr>
<tr><td></td><td colspan="2">Continue placement</td></tr>
<tr><td>Run student seminars</td><td>Attend seminars</td><td></td></tr>
<tr><td rowspan="3"></td><td colspan="2">Complete Charting Student Progress at the midway point</td></tr>
<tr><td colspan="2">Complete Charting Student Progress at the end of work experience</td></tr>
</table>

Table 1.1 Sequence of Activities in the Work-Based Learning Model *continued*

	EDUCATORS	STUDENTS	MENTORS	
Ensure open communication	**EVALUATION PHASE**			Continuing reflection
	Discuss students' learning and development with mentors	Students complete portfolio and self-assessment	Discuss students' learning and development with academics	
		Share work-based learning perceptions		
	Evaluate students			
	Reflect, revise, and enhance whole process			

However, while the activities required to facilitate such an interaction between the three worlds need to be carefully sequenced, an overall holistic view of the process must be maintained. "Boundaries" between the three worlds need to be seamless so that links and interactions between them are not impeded. Enhanced student learning occurs as a result of these interactions.

Many of the activities will be occurring at the same time so effective project management skills are essential for the person responsible for the implementation. In this model it is the educator. Also, at the beginning of the process, it is only the educators who have the overall holistic view or vision, and an important part of their responsibility is to ensure that this vision is shared and adopted by students and mentors. The preparation phase, where this shared vision is developed in students and mentors, is therefore an important part of the model and underpins the resultant successful outcomes.

The activities identified in table 1.1 have been categorized and listed according to the person primarily responsible for any associated action: the educator, the student, or the mentor. So, for example, all of the activities for which the educators have a responsibility are listed under the column heading "educators." Shaded areas indicate that no activity is required by that person at a particular time. The best overall understanding of the model and of the sequence of all of the activities can be gained by reading from the top left-hand corner of the table. Activities occurring concurrently are listed at the same level.

The following description based on table 1.1 is intended to provide only a brief overview of the model. Each aspect is explained in more detail in the following chapters. There are three phases to the model and each must be completed before the next one commences. The phases are the preparation phase, the experience phase, and the evaluation phase.

Preparation Phase

Where the model is being implemented for the first time educators must undertake some preliminary activities. Most importantly they must gain the support of their professional community, as the mentors will be drawn from this group. Educators also need to develop supporting materials and documentation for both students and mentors.

During the preparation phase, educators must identify potential students and mentors and run workshops for them. Although not the only purpose of these workshops, it is during this period that the shared vision begins to be developed.

Students and mentors meet and discuss specific goals and opportunities for the work experience. Students send mentors a copy of their curriculum vitae (CV), then mentors develop a draft plan of learning and discuss it with the student. The approval of the plan of learning concludes the preparation phase and the work experience itself can commence.

Experience Phase

The experience phase used by the authors and evaluated over a ten-year period requires students to attend the workplace for twelve months on a part-time basis. Initially, students complete a two-week block during a semester break and one full day for each teaching week of the following semester. This pattern is then repeated with students attending for another two-week block in the next semester break and one full day for each teaching week of the following semester. The pattern is illustrated in table 1.2.

Table 1.2 Typical Full-Time Course Pattern Incorporating Work-Based Learning

		Semester 1		Semester 2
	Year 1	Semester 1		Semester 2
		Course requirements		Course requirements
	Year 2	Semester 3		Semester 4
		Course requirements		Course requirements
Two-	Year 3	Semester 5	**Two-**	Semester 6
Week		Course requirements	**Week**	Course requirements
Block		**1 day per week**	**Block**	**1 day per week**
		work-based learning		**work-based learning**

Early in the experience phase, the educators visit each student and mentor in the workplace. This visit provides a "friendly" opportunity to see how the work-experience and mentoring relationship is progressing and to discuss issues of concern which may have arisen. Over the period of the actual work experience students also attend two seminars each semester as a group. During this period students develop a number of reflective learning strategies to enhance their overall learning experience.

Evaluation Phase

The final phase incorporates the student evaluation process and the evaluation of the model itself. The next chapter reviews the theory of experiential learning and the conditions under which such learning can be enhanced. Reflective thinking is an essential element of effective experiential learning.

2

Experiential Learning: Theory and Practice

Learning from experience is not a new educational concept, although the development of an applied theory to underpin such learning is more recent. The seminal work of David Kolb (1984) lays the foundations for contemporary interpretations and applications of experiential learning theory. Drawing upon the early thinkers in this field (John Dewey, Jean Piaget, and Kurt Lewin) Kolb concludes that a series of "propositions" underpin experiential learning. From each proposition, Kolb indicates an action which follows (represented in italic).

- Learning is best conceived as a process, not in terms of outcomes.
  Learning is continually modified by experience.

- Learning is a continuous process grounded in experience.
  Learning is testing and examining, then integrating new learning into what is known.

- The process of learning requires the resolution of conflicts between dialectically opposed modes of adaptation to the world.
  Learning is resolving conflicts between concrete experiences and abstract concepts; observation and action; the known and the unknown.

- Learning is an holistic process of adaptation to the world.
  Learning is a function of the total human interaction with the world, including thinking, feeling, perceiving, and behaving.

- Learning involves transactions between the person and the environment.
  Learning is an active and self-directed process.

- Learning is the process of creating knowledge.
  Learning is continuously refining and redefining knowledge.

Kolb proposes a definition of learning that usefully sums up the importance of learning through experience:

Learning is the process whereby knowledge is created through
the transformation of experience. (38)

Jack Mezirow and associates (1990) indicate the highly individual
nature of learning by defining it as

the process of making a new or revised interpretation of the
meaning of an experience, which guides subsequent understanding, appreciation, and action. (1)

Our learning, according to Mezirow and associates, is dependent
on the way we construct what our experience means. We are invariably
influenced firstly by our personal "perspectives," our values, theories,
and fundamental understandings (3). Secondly, we are influenced by
our "schemes," our expectations of cause-effect and if-then relationships (3). These perspectives and schemes, according to Mezirow and
associates, guide our interpretations of experience, and thus the final
outcomes of our learning from experience.

Although we cannot divorce ourselves entirely from these personal perspectives and schemes, we can subject our experience to reflective thinking and critical analysis. Thus our seemingly intractable
views of the world may be altered. Mezirow and associates suggest the
most significant learning experiences involve critical self-reflection,
"reassessing the way we have posed problems and reassessing our own
orientation to perceiving, knowing, believing, feeling, and action" (13).
Such "transformational" learning "leads to action that can significantly
affect the character of our interpersonal relationships, the organizations
in which we work and socialize, and the socioeconomic system itself"
(xiii).

Turning Experience into Learning

In order to understand the dynamic aspect of learning from experience,
David Boud's model usefully outlines three stages: preparation, experience, and reflective processes.

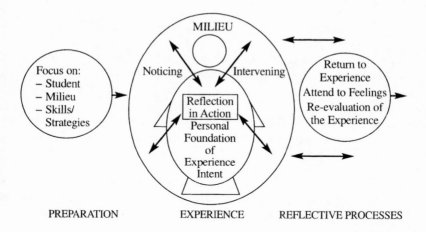

Figure 2.1 Model of Learning from Experience (Boud 1993)

During the preparation stage represented by the firstcircle, the following aspects must be considered:

- the learner—what background does the learner bring to the experience?

- the milieu—what does the experience offer?

- learning strategies—what knowledge and skills does the learner bring to the experience?

During the experience, as represented by the middle oval, learners interact with the organization, staff, events, and all that takes place. They learn by observing and participating and by *intervening* and *influencing* what is taking place.

The third circle, the reflective processes, suggests learners return to the experience, recall feelings, and reevaluate the experience.

Creating the Climate for Reflective Learning

So how can tertiary educators facilitate reflecting on experience as outlined above? David Boud, Rosemary Keogh, and David Walker (1985a) suggest the overall role which educators can play is "to provide a context and a space to learn, give support and encouragement, listen to the learner and provide access to particular devices which may be of use" (38).

Reflecting on learning experiences does not come naturally and intuitively for many people. Yet, the process of reflecting can be facilitated. David Boud and Susan Knights (1994) suggest some of the following can create a conducive climate for reflective learning:

- explain the rationale for reflective learning
- illustrate the process through exercises
- provide opportunities to clarify understanding of reflection
- introduce a model or framework for thinking about reflection
- model the approach to reflective thinking
- encourage students to take control of the process
- provide time for reflection
- encourage having a "reflective partner" to share reflections on experiences
- maintain journals for reflective thoughts and reevaluate these
- introduce reflective reports which demonstrate learning achievements

Boud and his colleagues have explored extensively the field of experiential learning over the last two decades. They were particularly interested in what turns experience into learning. Their view is that *reflection* is the key (Boud, Keogh, and Walker 1985a). *Reflection* is defined as "a generic term for those intellectual and affective activities in which individuals engage to explore their experiences in order to lead to new understandings and appreciations." Reflection involves three stages in which learners must engage for effective learning. Each of these stages includes an example from practice. "Andrew" represents a student using the three stages of reflection on experience. His experiences are commented upon by the educators in the examples below.

Stage 1: Returning to the Experience

Stage 1 involves recalling the events, replaying of the initial experience, and recounting the experience.

Returning to the experience can be achieved by reviewing the experience and writing about it or describing it to others. At this stage, a nonjudgmental chronological description of the experience elicits the details and recreates the experience afresh. Feelings, thoughts, and actions of the individuals involved at the time are all important recollections. Both positive and negative aspects should be part of the recollection.

Example of Stage 1

Andrew is a confident and articulate student and is keen to participate in his internship. He has a tendency to take on too many extra-curricular activities and occasionally misses important deadlines or promises more than he can deliver. During the early part of his internship, Andrew agreed to research information for a report associated with an important project at his workplace. He missed the deadline. Afterward, Andrew talked about his experience during a class seminar, reviewing what led to his missing the deadline and the excruciating meeting with details of the conversation between himself and his mentor.

Stage 2: Attending to Feelings

Stage 2 involves the conscious recall of good experiences and associated pleasurable feelings and those experiences with negative associations.

Attending to feelings provides the opportunity to consider the effects, both positive and negative, that feelings may have had on past and future learning experiences. Focusing on the good experiences recalls positive feelings that can be marshaled as approaches to future learning. Similarly, facing experiences that were less successful and recalling associated feelings can enable negative feelings to be faced and mechanisms for addressing these to be developed.

Example of Stage 2

Andrew talked about his personal embarrassment, his mentor's disappointment in him, and his own fear that he had damaged his reputation. He knew that meeting deadlines and managing his time were his personal problems, and he recalled further examples during his course of study and personal life. Andrew believed that unless he developed strategies to overcome these problems, he would certainly be damaging his professional career. Andrew knew that when he *did* perform, he felt really proud of himself. His university lecturers often talked to Andrew about his "potential" and his recurring problems, and they offered a number of strategies he might try to overcome them.

Stage 3: Reevaluating Experience

Stage 3 involves the review and evaluation of experience and associating the experience and knowledge gained with what is already known.

Reevaluating experience incorporates time between the experience, as outlined in stages 1 and 2. This final stage involves identifying the outcomes of the learning. Boud, Keogh, and Walker (1985a) identify four aspects which will enhance the learning experience: association, relating the new to what is already known; seeking relationships between the data; testing ideas and feelings; and, finally, owning that knowledge personally.

Example of Stage 3

At the conclusion of the internship, all the students were invited to talk about the "highs and lows" of their work-based learning and to share two items from their collection of achievements and related reflections on their learning (included in their portfolio). Andrew described this incident as the most important one of his internship. He recognized his future career was very important to him, and he knew the further study he was planning made a change essential. He outlined his strategies for deciding just how much he could handle and do well and techniques for managing his time better. The two items from his portfolio demonstrated tasks that were completed in a timely and efficient manner with accompanying praise from his mentor. When reviewing his internship with the educator, Andrew's mentor described a positive change in Andrew after this incident.

The advantage of this detailed recall is that all related experiences can be collected, and the perceptions of others on the same experience can be added to the collective view. Expressing these experiences in writing or orally serves to clarify, extend, and enhance the memories. Mere reflection will not in itself lead to enhanced learning from experience. The most successful reflection incorporates a resulting action or commitment to action. Learners must, ultimately, make these reflections and learn from them, but they are assisted by both educators and mentors in the workplace.

The next chapter examines strategies which have proved useful for students in developing reflective thinking and learning skills.

3

Strategies for Enhancing Student Learning

During the ten years' operation of the model, particular strategies have proved useful in bringing together the three worlds of learning. Some strategies are designed for students to use on their own in developing their reflective thinking learning skills. Some strategies are designed for use in the workplace with the mentor and student working together. A final group of strategies is designed for group interaction in seminar sessions where students work with each other and with the educator. The aim of all these strategies is to enhance students' learning through work-based experience by bringing together the world of student experience, the world of tertiary professional education, and the world of work-based learning.

Educators' Support of Students' Learning and Reflection

As students begin their work-based learning experiences, they often lack confidence. They may be experiencing difficulties, but are unable to pinpoint their problems or work out ways to solve these. They may be confused by particular work practices or concerned over workplace interpersonal conflict. They may wonder why work practices and theory learned in their professional course seem to disagree. Here the educators play a very important role in assisting students to reflect upon what they are learning and what that learning means. But reflection does not come easily to many. C. C. Johns (1994) argues that individuals require coaching and supervision when developing skills of reflection. In this model, students need support in developing their reflective skills to make connections between their own personal knowledge base, what they are learning in their tertiary studies, and what they are experiencing in the workplace.

Practicing Reflective Learning

New learning situations invariably make students uneasy. They wonder, What will be expected of me? Will I be able to perform satisfactorily? What if I don't know the answer or don't know how to do something? Such concerns can be shared between students engaged in work-based experience. In this model, group seminars are held on campus four times over the year. These have proved invaluable in supporting students. Their moments of shared disquiet and exhilaration are invariably of great interest to other students and act as motivators for further learning.

Without the educator's guidance, discussion of students' work-based experiences can result in simple recounts of what happened. Hazel Platzer, Jannice Snelling, and David Blake (1997), when examining models and frameworks for facilitating reflection on learning, found that a variety of strategies were required to match learners' individual approaches to learning. Educators are particularly important here. They are familiar with the students, and they are also trained listeners and facilitators. During seminars, educators can enter the discussion at appropriate moments, facilitating students' analyses of their experiences. Students can be encouraged to remove themselves momentarily from a particular experience and to review it as an outside observer. Replaying that experience, they can then reconsider their reactions, including how they felt, and develop new insights, awareness, or understanding of the experience. With the educators' guidance, such experiences can be linked to both academic studies and the students' personal world of experience.

Remembering the necessity to use several different approaches to facilitate reflective learning, the following strategies have proved useful:

- individual students report and reflect on their experiences through sharing a journal entry of their choice
- students discuss and reflect on their experiences with a supportive partner
- students as a group collectively reflect on their experiences presented, thus gaining multiple perspectives on these

In the initial seminar session, students tend to hold back their own reflections until they feel it is "safe" to share their responses. They worry that they have little to contribute to the group's understanding.

Here the educator can facilitate a nonjudgmental atmosphere, mutual trust, and a sense of community amongst members of the group. Once a supportive environment is created, members of the group can elicit further details on the individuals' experiences. They might probe comments made, query responses exchanged, question body language used, examine arguments presented and defended, review emotions expressed, consider problems solved, and pose resolutions. These multiple perspectives can provide additional reflections and insights into the experience.

To learn from experience, learners must to be attuned to what is happening. Educators can assist students in becoming more skilled in the reflective process by encouraging them to use questions, making notes after important incidents, reviewing and reflecting on any records of events. Typical questions include:

- What happened?
- Why might this have happened?
- How was this matter resolved?

Recording and Reflecting in Journals

One of the most personalized and powerful ways students can reflect upon their learning is by keeping a journal. It must be more than a simple recall of events. Students should view it as a record of their personal "journey" and their reflections upon that journey at different times along the way.

Those who have not used journals before might question their value and worry that journals are a totally new form of expression for them. To ease this sense of the unfamiliar, Rebecca O'Rourke (1998) suggests comparing journals with the familiar essay. Both focus on the student's understanding of a body of knowledge. Both require the student to think critically about that knowledge and its uses. Both require students to communicate their insights. Put this way, the journal seems more familiar.

Some wonder what should be recorded in a journal and how to get started. Peter November (1996) suggests using an "agenda prompt" which identifies current issues and subtopics of these issues and suggests possible outcomes, action to be taken, and reflections on performance with this issue (123). Helen Woodward (1998) suggests a framework to guide students' journal entries that signals what is important to convey and how to use that information. Woodward suggests using a "double-entry" format where the left-hand column is used to record experiences, notes, quotations, and so on, and the right-hand side is used to record reflections on these. Where appropriate, such reflections may conclude with a suggested action.

Graham Gibbs (1995) suggests ways that reflections recorded in the journals can prove useful. They can be used for

- private records for review and reflection
- discussion between mentor and learner
- discussion between learner and educator
- discussion between others associated with learning experiences
- sharing in group situations
- retrospective personal evaluation of learning experiences

Just as guidance would be given for writing essays, so there should be guidance on style, tone, inclusions, and exclusions for the journal. These guidelines should be discussed with the students, with significant input from the students regarding what might be included. Items to include in journals suggested by Keith Morrison (1996) provide a useful start for this discussion, including

- comments, reflections, and evaluations of experience
- reactions to personal reading and study habits
- personal objectives and how these have been achieved
- expectations, attitudes, values, beliefs, knowledge, and skills
- significant events, reflections, decisions, insights, evaluations, and views
- comments on relationships between professional practice, academic work, and personal development
- changes and developments in professional practice

Two particular issues arise with the use of journals. The first concerns whether journals should be shared and, if so, with whom? This model suggests that students voluntarily share their journals during seminars and with their mentors and educators as opportunities and needs arise. The second issue involves whether journals should be assessed or not. The model under discussion does not assess the journals, given their main purpose here is to encourage students' personal reflection. Should the decision to assess journals be made,

O'Rourke (1998) highlights the importance of establishing criteria for assessing them and conveying these to the students. Ultimately, the decision whether or not to share and assess journals is one of individual judgment. In deciding whether or not to assess journals, it is helpful to consider the journal's purpose and whether it is

- appropriate for judging the learning outcomes of the particular course
- intended to support learning, provide evidence of learning, induce reflection on experience, or teach learning from experience
- optional or integral to assessable activity
- a record of personal growth and development for individual reflection
- a record of personal growth and development for assessment

There is one further point regarding journals. Some students find reflecting upon themselves in a personal journal an unnatural and difficult task despite all the supporting discussion of concerns. There are other strategies for reflection which can be just as effective. These include producing a portfolio and engaging in self-assessment. This model proposes that all three—journal, portfolio, and self-assessment—make a useful contribution towards creating a reflective learner. Such a learner uses these to make links between the three worlds of learning.

Providing Evidence of Learning through Portfolios

The journal is an ongoing record of learning and reflection on that learning. Portfolios are designed to provide tangible, concrete evidence that learning has taken place. While this model does not assess the student's journal, the portfolio has formed a useful part of the final assessment of work-based learning.

Portfolios have been widely used in creative arts subjects where students collect their "best work" to demonstrate their talents, knowledge, and skills. Purposes of portfolios are many, but for work-based learning experiences, they mainly assist students in reflecting on and assessing their personal goals and achievements (Gibbs 1995; Nightingale, Wiata, Toohey, Ryan, Hughes, and Magin 1997). Most importantly, portfolios should demonstrate that students know *what* and *how* learning has occurred. Woodward (1998) also suggests that since they are the student's record of what they consider important, then they offer others a helpful perspective on the student's learning.

Guidelines for developing portfolios such as the ones below should be provided to students. Guidelines should indicate the

- clear rationale for the portfolio
- kinds of content to be collected
- scope and breadth of the collection, including maximum and minimum sizes
- selection, rationale, and match of learning objectives to included materials
- requirements for reflective commentary
- suggestions for organizing and indexing the portfolio

In preparing students for developing their portfolios, it is helpful to outline a four-step process that involves

- outlining goals of work-based learning experience
- setting the criteria for inclusion of material
- selecting the "evidence" relevant to these criteria
- making a judgment about the extent to which the criteria have been met

When portfolios are a new concept for students, it is useful to suggest the type of materials they might include such as

- statements about their personal objectives
- examples of how these objectives have been realized
- analysis of understandings gleaned from student group discussion
- examples of work produced and commentary on learning outcomes
- material which demonstrates learning has occurred and has been consolidated within their own world of knowledge
- understandings at a theoretical level examples of enhanced generic skills
- examples of skills gained that are relevant to career or profession

Students often have difficulty deciding what they should say about their selected materials. In making their selection of materials, students have reasons why the item is important. These reasons should form the basis for considering what will be useful to say. Students could be encouraged to write about

- evolving thought processes
- dealing with emotions felt and demonstrated in the workplace
- understanding of organizational culture
- "roads" taken, including dead ends, alternative routes taken, and important arrival points
- decision-making moments
- strategies for developing competencies in new skills and knowledge
- applications of newly acquired skills or knowledge

Examining Learning through Self-Assessment

Portfolios require students to collect materials throughout the work experience so that there is tangible evidence of learning and reflection. A related strategy is self-assessment which can be appropriately used at the conclusion of work-based learning experiences. There are a number of similarities between portfolios and self-assessment. The major difference used in this model is that self-assessment requires a concluding or summative reflection on all that has been learned, whereas the portfolio is used for collecting materials that reflect learning still in the developing or formative stage.

According to Boud (1991), self-assessment

requires students to think critically about what they are learning, to identify appropriate standards of performance and to apply them to their own work. Self-assessment encourages students to look to themselves and to other sources to determine what criteria should be used in judging their work rather than being dependent solely on their teachers or other authorities. (1)

Statements of self-assessment should typically include a projection of future learning, building on what has gone on before. Self-assessment is all about looking closely at oneself and

- developing, monitoring, and assessing one's own learning
- achieving individual goals
- planning future learning experiences

The ability to undertake self-assessment is a valuable life-long learning skill (Boud 1995). It can empower the individual and ensure learning experiences are more meaningful. Despite its value, there is resistance. Valeria Clifford (1999) found that many students find self-assessment "foreign" and difficult, and contend that assessment is the educator's responsibility (123). Thus Clifford suggests it is necessary to provide some guidance in understanding what self-assessment entails and how it can be done.

Several studies indicate that the ability to self-assess can be developed through feedback on learning and through practice over time (Boud and Falchikov 1989; Birenbaum and Douchy 1996). F. Douchy, M. Segers, and D. Sluijsman (1999) conclude from their review of the literature that self-assessment is facilitated by discussion and exercises. In this model, feedback, practice, discussion, and exercises are all incorporated into the various strategies such as the assessment of personal, technical, and professional skills, journal, portfolio, and monitoring development during the work-based learning experience.

It is the students who are responsible for self-assessment. There are others though who contribute to the student's process of self-assessment. Mentors provide opportunities for student learning and continuously monitor how well that learning is going. Educators assist through managing all aspects of the model. Students interact in seminars and at other times informally thus assisting each other to gain insights into their learning.

Douchy, Segers, and Sluijsman (1999) indicate that the literature revealed effective self-assessment focuses students and enables them to

- set out objectives and tasks for themselves
- indicate how these would be judged (establish criteria)
- understand "good and bad" characteristics of work produced
- provide examples of evidence that these objectives have been met
- make comments on how well these objectives have been met
- indicate further action necessary to meet these objectives
- suggest future goals which build upon those achieved
- show evidence of taking responsibility for their own learning

Self-assessment is particularly valuable because it focuses students' learning at all stages—before the learning experience begins, during the learning experience, and at the conclusion of the learning experience. It sets clear goals for everyone concerned with the experience, including the mentors who have the task of identifying and designing appropriate learning activities in consultation with students and the educators. In a sense the student is saying, "Here is what I'd like to know, my evidence that learning has happened, my record of how that happened, and when everything didn't go as planned, what I did to ensure that learning happened."

At the conclusion of a work-based learning experience, self-assessment provides the culminating reflective exercise. Learners should reexamine and reflect upon their journals and portfolios and their Charting Student Progress Guide. Considering these items in conjunction should provide insights into the three worlds of learning so that connections can be made between these worlds.

Some of the elements which might be included in self-assessment statements include:

- an overview which brings together the range of learning that has occurred and self-reflection on that learning
- personal goals pursued as well as those of the mentors, other supervisors, and educators
- extent to which these goals have been achieved
- how the goals have been reached, and how the student knows these goals have been reached
- evidence that demonstrates achievements
- concluding statement that highlights overall learning outcomes

Some of the evidence that might be cited in the self-assessment includes:

- journal entries
- reflections on portfolio items
- comments from the educator, mentor, or other work-based supervisor
- proof of new insights
- evidence of enhanced skills
- evidence of changed attitudes
- statement about the extent and quality of personal achievements
- "next steps" planned to continue the learning experiences

Douchy, Segers, and Sluijsman (1999) indicate the strengths of self-assessment for student learning. It promotes the learning of skills and abilities, leads to increased self-reflection, promotes a higher standard of outcomes, enhances one's responsibility for one's own learning and increases the use of problem-solving strategies.

Moving beyond Personal Reflection

Dochy, Segers, and Sluijsman (1999) point out that case-based and problem-based learning are particularly valuable for learning in real-life contexts. The workplace provides an ideal environment, a "real-life context," through which students can enhance their critical thinking and problem-solving skills (332). This model recommends using case studies, role plays, and problem-based learning as effective strategies for enhancing work-based learning experiences. Such strategies enable individuals to understand more complex interactions and issues and to consider how they themselves might have handled such interactions or resolved such issues.

Using Case Studies

Work-based learning alone cannot offer a sufficiently broad range of scenarios to prepare students for the real workplace. For example, complex workplace events or interpersonal exchanges can be difficult to view from all perspectives, and all contributing aspects may not be evident. Unpleasant or threatening scenarios may be difficult to examine dispassionately or "from a distance." In these instances, prepared case studies can capture the range of emotions, represent opposing sides of issues, and replay particular conflicts and scenarios. These then can be isolated for scrutiny, discussion, and consideration of a range of possible solutions. They are ideal material for seminar inter-action.

Most areas of professional education have published case studies which can be used or adapted. Specially created case studies offer materials that can be tailor-made in terms of content, length, and style. In developing this model, for example, case studies were developed which tackled particular issues which students found difficult to understand (Alderman and Milne, assisted by Gemmell 1997). Once appropriate case studies are created or selected, there are many ways to use them. A formal presentation and discussion of the case study may follow these steps:

- identify the problem/issue
- describe the context surrounding the problem/issue
- identify criteria for selecting solutions
- generate alternative solutions and identifying implications of these
- select, evaluate, and implement the solution
- review the solution

Generally, the solution to the "problem" is less important than the discussion and decision-making processes used to reach the solution.

Using Role Plays

Case studies can appear rigid. Often the details of the scenario, players, responses, and the outcomes have all been "prearranged" by the author of the case study. For more creative opportunities to observe, reflect, and discuss possibilities, role plays can be very effective.

They provide a way to feel like a player rather than an observer. The inbuilt air of spontaneity of role plays promotes a free exchange of views often not possible in a case study. Their unpredictable responses mirror what goes on in the real world. While the roles played may be exaggerated to highlight a particular issue, the wide range of roles possible makes the boundaries of the situation very flexible and inter-action seemingly more realistic.

The educator acting as the role play facilitator should

- incorporate desired issues
- identify the major issues for consideration
- feature sufficient roles to explore the issues
- set the scene by describing the scenario
- assign roles to be played
- describe how the role play will proceed
- describe how and when the role play will be concluded
- debrief participants after the role play has concluded

This final point is especially important. After participants air a range of views and consider various perspectives, the facilitator should assist them to "step outside" their roles. It is very easy to become totally immersed in the role played. Participants also need the opportunity to reflect upon the scenario, to consider what has transpired and what this means, as an external observer. At this stage, it is important to encourage students to consider their own personal reactions and how the role play may have provided new insights for them personally. Reflecting upon learning experiences is a means to an end—to consolidate experience into changed thinking or behavior.

Tackling Problem-Based Learning

Problem-based learning (PBL) is another student-centered learning strategy which is ideally suited to both individual and group experiential learning. PBL places problems, queries, or puzzles particular to the profession at the center of learning. Course content revolves around these. David Boud and Grahame Feletti (1997) define PBL as "an approach to structuring the curriculum which involves confronting students with problems from practice which provide a stimulus for learning" (5).

Problem-based learning is a particularly useful educator's strategy for professional education courses. PBL's particular advantages are that it

- recognizes the impossibility of learning all there is to know in a professional field
- begins at the student's stage of knowledge
- adapts to different students' levels of ability and understanding and the sharing of these different understandings
- develops a range of valuable generic skills: critical thinking, problem-solving, research, and oral and written communication
- facilitates continual updating of course material
- enables course content to be adaptable and flexible in incorporating new concepts
- enables theory and practice to be more closely aligned

There is an important aspect to PBL which distinguishes it from the usual teaching and learning practices in tertiary education. Bob Ross (1997) suggests that traditionally

it is assumed that students have to have the knowledge required
to approach a problem before they can start on the problem; here
[PBL] the knowledge arises from work on the problem. (30)

Most commonly, PBL forms the basis of teaching and learning for a complete subject or an entire course. It can equally provide focus for examining work-based learning practices. Problem-based learning involves standard procedures (based on Boud and Feletti 1997; Woods 1985; Ross 1997):

- learning objectives are identified
- problem is presented, before preparation or formal study has occurred
- problem is presented as it would appear in "real life"
- students work with the problem, applying critical thinking and problem-solving skills to identify aspects of the problem
- students identify information required to explore aspects of the problem
- students apply research skills to find, evaluate, and analyze material relevant to the problem
- students communicate their findings
- students critically review and recast their findings
- students demonstrate how the problem links to and consolidates their existing knowledge

The reasoning behind the selection of the problem is very important here. Ross (1997) suggests the problem can be selected to

- cover a predefined area of knowledge
- learn a set of concepts, ideas, techniques
- highlight parts of the field of knowledge
- present a problem of intrinsic interest or importance
- represent typical problems faced by the profession

How then can PBL be implemented? Boud and Feletti (1997) suggest

- using stimulus material to help students discuss an important problem, question, or issue within the body of professional knowledge and practice
- presenting the problem as a simulation of professional practice or a "real life" situation
- guiding students' critical thinking and providing resources to help them learn the process of defining and resolving problems
- having students work cooperatively as a group, exploring information with access to a tutor who knows the problem well and can facilitate the group's learning process

- getting students to identify their own information needs and appropriate use of resources
- reapplying this new knowledge to the original problems and evaluating their learning processes

The role of the tutor in problem-based learning has proved to be very important. Graham D. Hendry, Miriam Frommer, and Richard A. Walker (1999) advise that tutors should interject with questions when interest wanes or discussion looses focus. They may ask students to recall existing knowledge and its applicability to the particular problem under consideration. Tutors may lead students to reflect on their problem-solving strategy, that is reflect on their thinking process. Tutors mainly act as facilitators and guides, rather than as directors of learning.

The next chapter examines facilitated mentoring as an essential ingredient of the model. The requisite element is a mentor who becomes an active partner in designing and facilitating learning experiences to ensure quality learning outcomes for the student.

4

Facilitated Mentoring: Enhancing Student-Centered Learning

The world of work-based learning experiences is the aspect of the model where the student and the mentor interact within the context of the mentor's organization. When the student/workplace supervisor relationship is based on a facilitated mentoring model, enhanced learning outcomes are the result. Engaging the mentor as an active partner in designing the learning experience produces a synergy that is a very powerful ingredient in the process. However, although great attention has been paid to both informal and facilitated mentoring relationships since the mid-1970s, particularly in the world of business, using expert practitioners to mentor students as part of tertiary professional education has been little explored (Murray 1991).

Mentoring itself is not new. History gives many examples of the value of mentoring, and these same principles have been key elements in the continuity of art, craft, and commerce from ancient times. The master/apprentice relationship of the Middle Ages was eventually transformed into the employer/employee relationship by industrial society.

The mentoring relationship requires more of workplace supervisors than simply providing projects for the students to work on or day-to-day supervision of students on the job. It implies taking students into organizations as members of workplace teams, assisting their socialization into the organizations, devising plans that facilitate customized learning experiences, and giving feedback that will allow students to reflect on their own learning and development. It also presupposes a commitment to the students' personal and professional development. In effect, it is recreating the master/apprentice relationship of the Middle Ages. The apprentice (student) is socialized into the profession at the same time as learning the "skills of the trade," or in this case, the "tenets of the profession."

Mentoring describes a particular system of communication using a specific set of skills and body of knowledge, tailor-made for a particular arrangement between mentors and students (Fisher 1994).

It implies a certain arrangement between the individuals. Each arrangement will be unique, its particular nature created by the personalities of
the two people concerned. However, in itself, mentoring is a learning
process because it is part of a system in which people engage when life
presents them with situations for which they are not prepared (Fisher
1994). A. Mumford (1987) concludes at the end of his study into
management development processes that incidental learning occurs
when new situations are dealt with. He also notes that the additional
help which trusted mentors offer is a valuable asset in the learning
process.

A committed mentor can assist learning in many ways, but most
significantly by encouraging students to participate in reflective thinking and critical analysis. At its most effective, the mentoring relationship follows the Socratic method. Having an overall conceptual picture
and using the Socratic process of questioning, mentors are able to lead
students' thinking processes so the students ultimately are able to
engage with the mentors' conceptual worlds.

Good mentors will not judge or instruct; they will facilitate or
interpret and empower students to arrive at their own decisions and
conclusions. They will allow the students to take risks, but be there for
them to provide ongoing support where necessary. "Support" and
"challenge" have been identified as the two factors which are most
critical to the creation of successful relationships when supervisors are
helping students to learn (Daloz 1986). While "support" affirms the
students and lets them know they are cared about, "challenge" puts
pressure on them and emphasizes the gap between what they are
capable of at present and what they need to be capable of in the future.
This theory suggests that students can perceive different mixtures of
support and challenge in their workplace experience.

The best mixture, resulting in students achieving growth in learning, is a high amount of support combined with a high amount of
challenge. Where students feel they receive high support but low
challenge, they will feel affirmed and cared about, but not stimulated to
learn any more. Students who feel low support and low challenge are
likely to experience a state of stasis where learning grinds to a standstill
and they mark time. The worst combination of all for the student is that
of high challenge and low support. Students who feel their supervision
is like this are likely to retreat from the situation and even walk away.

It is also important that mentors maintain a professional balance in
their relationship with students. The mentor/student relationship can be

viewed on a spectrum that extends from the highly personal at one end to the highly professional at the other. The best position on this spectrum is somewhere towards the middle, but positioned slightly more on the professional side of the spectrum. The best description of the relationship in these terms would be as "professionally friendly."

While examples of mentoring in the literature reflect both formal and informal arrangements, where mentoring is an integral component of professional education in a tertiary environment, a structured model is desirable (Murray 1991). In a tertiary environment, it is important that the model enables a process for evaluating and assessing the student. Murray's model of facilitated mentoring is defined as

> a deliberate pairing of a more skilled or experienced person with a lesser skilled or experienced one, with the agreed upon goal of having the lesser skilled person grow and develop provides such a structure.

A work-based learning experience that utilizes a facilitated mentoring model provides

> a structure and series of processes designed to create effective mentoring relationships, guide the desired behavior change of those involved, and evaluate the results. (Murray 1991, 5)

This type of mentoring requires a mentor and a student to enter into an overt agreement to interact in certain ways to facilitate the learning, growth, and skill development of the student. Facilitated mentoring includes

- an educator responsible for maintaining the program and supporting the relationships
- criteria and a process for selecting the students
- diagnosing the developmental needs of students
- criteria and a process for selecting mentors
- orientation to the responsibilities of the role for both mentors and students
- strategies for matching mentors and students on the basis of compatibility and skills to be developed
- a negotiated agreement between mentor and student

- formative evaluation to make any necessary adjustments to the program
- summative evaluation to determine outcomes for the students, mentors, academics, the profession and the tertiary institution

Although Murray's model distinguishes between the roles of mentor and that of role model (viewed as an unstructured, informal relationship), the latter should naturally become an important component of the student/workplace supervisor mentoring relationship. Role modeling implies a senior or more experienced person setting a desirable example and the student identifying with it. It is both a conscious and an unconscious process. Interaction around organizational tasks, common organizational concerns, and larger career issues is a conscious modeling process. Through it, the students learn approaches, attitudes, and values held by the models, who, in turn, have the opportunity to articulate central parts of their self-images in the work role. Models shape students' style, personal values, and professional identity. As students develop and mature, they may continue to emulate certain aspects of the models' style while rejecting others. As this process occurs, the students develop a clearer sense of who they are (Kram 1988).

The adopted definition of mentoring may imply that all benefits are directed towards the students (Murray 1991). However, mentoring provides benefits to mentors as well. Studies such as those of D. J. Levinson and others (1978) and J. G. Clawson (1980) show that in helping a person establish a place in the world of work, an individual benefits from providing support and guidance. Mentors review and reappraise the past as they participate in students' attempts to face the challenges of professional life. In so doing, they gain internal satisfaction and respect for their capabilities as teachers or advisers.

As well as personal satisfaction, Fisher (1994) highlights other benefits for mentors. By clarifying and articulating ideas for others, mentors gain experience in strategic thinking in a considerable variety of situations beyond their own immediate experiences. The one-to-one nature of mentoring which allows quality time with another person inevitably leads to a greater understanding of oneself and one's motives, leading to a reevaluation of one's personal philosophy.

As students develop competence, mentors' acceptance and confirmation provide support and encouragement. Conversely, as the mentors strive to feel useful and creative, the acceptance and confirmation offered by the students provide support for the wisdom and experience offered by the mentors to the next generation of professionals. This relationship of acceptance and confirmation enables the students to experiment with new behaviors. The basic trust provided by the relationship encourages students to take risks and to venture into unfamiliar ways of relating to the professional environment.

The qualities a mentor should possess include:

- intelligence and integrity
- professional knowledge and skills
- professional attitude
- high personal standards
- enthusiasm
- willingness to share accumulated knowledge

There is no formula for the role of the mentor in this type of learning experience. Depending on the two people involved, the workplace, and the nature of the work undertaken, mentors fulfill some combination of the following roles:

- facilitator
- counselor
- adviser
- guide
- coordinator
- assessor
- role model
- opener of doors
- confidant
- communicator
- bridge
- link
- partner
- friend

In performing these roles, mentors gain through

- participation in students' personal and professional growth thereby receiving intrinsic satisfaction through a sharing of professional skills and knowledge
- enhanced ability to impart skills and knowledge which may further career development
- collaboration in the production of skilled, competent, and leading-edge professionals for the workplace
- opportunities to assess students for future employment
- exposure to current literature and "best practices" through interaction with students and educators
- collaboration with educators to address workplace problems and issues
- enhanced analytical and strategic thinking skills through clarifying thoughts and ideas for another
- greater understanding of oneself and human nature through re-evaluation of personal philosophy and professional values (Fisher 1994)

Some recent research has examined student perceptions of the way they are supervised during work experience (Cameron-Jones and O'Hara 1999). Based on a theoretical model developed by Laurent A. Daloz (1986), Cameron-Jones and O'Hara studied a population of almost six hundred students in four teacher training courses in the UK to explore these students' perceptions. Their research findings were congruent with Daloz's theory.

Results showed that the kind of supervision most frequently perceived by students as "best" was one that offered high degrees of support with high degrees of challenge. In addition, student perception of the type of supervision they received affected their overall level of satisfaction with the experience, and there was a strong correlation between students' actual and predicted (based on their perceptions of their supervision experience) dropout rates.

Cameron-Jones and O'Hara also asked students to rate their perceptions of the extent to which their supervisors played supportive roles (friend, supporter, intermediary, and door-opener) and challenging roles (model, assessor, coach, and standard-prodder). Findings showed that students saw the roles of supporter and model as featuring most strongly in what their supervisors did for them.

The outcomes of this research have strong implications for the mentor/student relationship and consequent student learning. Mentors should strive to create a learning environment that both supports and challenges the students.

However, despite the best efforts of all concerned, unexpected problems can occur. If they do, it becomes the responsibility of the educator, who may need to intervene on behalf of the student. The practical application of the model discusses mechanisms to ensure that the world of work-based learning provides a learning experience that both supports and challenges the student.

Over the ten years of implementing this model of work-based learning, the authors have collected much anecdotal evidence that supports the Daloz theory of supervision in work-based learning and the research conducted by Cameron-Jones and O'Hara. Some mentoring relationships and their outcomes for student learning, which are typical of the many anecdotes collected, are described in the following examples.

High Support/Low Challenge

One mentor offered so much support that she moved the relationship too far towards the personal end of the professional/personal mentoring relationship spectrum. She "mothered" the student and created an over-dependence on the part of the student that inhibited learning.

The student was affirmed and felt cared about but was not stimulated to learn.

Low Support/Low Challenge

One student was given low-level repetitious tasks instead of the professionally challenging ones that had been agreed upon. This can also occur if the mentor is too busy to give the necessary time to the mentoring relationship and it becomes easier to merely direct the student to complete low-level tasks which do not require any assistance or guidance from the mentor. When selecting mentors, educators should not choose mentors whose own workload is "over-heavy." Very little supervision and feedback was provided by the mentor to the student.

Student learning ground to a standstill. The student became disappointed and bored and felt that his time was being wasted.

High Challenge/Low Support

A student was expected to operate independently, at quite a high level of professionalism, in an isolated environment where she had little contact with her mentor and also had no regular daily contact with anyone else in the organization.

The student developed (quite reasonably), feelings of personal and professional inadequacy and considered giving up her studies as a direct result. It was a potentially damaging situation for the student and required direct intervention by the educator.

High Challenge/High Support

A student working in a national archiving agency was given the task of describing and arranging a large collection of papers donated by one of Australia's leading historians.

The student reached an exceptionally high level of intellectual and professional achievement. Using the Socratic method, her mentor constantly challenged her. Through his questioning techniques she developed important strategies for problem solving. At the end of the experience she recognized that her whole approach to problem solving, at the personal as well as the professional level, had been transformed.

What characteristics make a good mentor? Fisher (1994) provides a checklist highlighting features that characterize "good" and "bad" mentors.

Good Mentors	Bad Mentors
1. Permissive not authoritarian	Too directive
2. Well informed	Opinionated
3. Analytical	Dogmatic
	Negative
4. Commitment to training	Place no value on training
5. Commitment to development	No interest in development of staff
6. Good communicators	Poor communicators
7. Good open questioners	Use closed questions
8. Good listeners	Poor listeners
9. Good knowledge of organization	Knowledge limited to department/section
10. Can apply theory to practice	Not really well educated, no real understanding of theory
11. Well organized	Disorganized

In this model of work-based learning, the workplace supervisors, or mentors, are active partners with educators in designing students' learning experiences. The mentors' contributions are based on sound professional practice and motivated by a commitment to the profession. Mentors share with educators the responsibility for facilitating student learning and development. Through their relationships with students, mentors facilitate many of the reflective learning strategies and processes described in chapter 3. This type of collaboration can only be achieved if educators and mentors share the same vision for the outcomes. The most effective way to ensure that a shared vision does exist is to require the mentors to attend workshop sessions prior to the commencement of the program. The suggested content for such sessions and other issues related to the practical application of the model are outlined in chapter 6.

5

Monitoring Levels of Learners' Achievement and Evaluating the Model

Developing and implementing a work-based learning program that features reflective learning strategies and facilitated mentoring can be a daunting task. How can those involved ensure that learning outcomes are being achieved? This chapter discusses strategies to monitor and evaluate students' achievements and those which ensure the model itself is effective.

Evaluating Learning Outcomes of the Student

Monitoring Learning in the Workplace—Educator's Visits

The plan of learning is crucial to a successful work-based learning experience. It outlines the work areas where learning will occur, tasks to be learned, strategies to achieve these learning outcomes, and how the learning will be supervised. To ensure that the experience is working effectively, the tertiary educator should meet with both student and mentor in the workplace shortly after a predetermined block of initial time. The purpose of this visit is to

- clarify any points of concern
- check that the plan is being implemented
- discuss the initial review of the learner's performance
- reconfirm the educator as a point of contact
- determine whether learner or mentor needs additional support

This initial contact confirms the importance of the collaborative efforts of student, educator, and mentor and sets the scene for a co-operative relationship.

Monitoring Learning in the Workplace—Student Seminars

A series of student seminars, facilitated by the educators and spaced out over the length of the work-based learning program, is an essential feature of the model. These seminars provide opportunities for students to reflect on their learning through various educators' strategies such as case studies, role plays, and problem-based learning. These strategies are discussed in chapter 3. Most importantly, the seminars provide opportunities throughout the work-based learning to confirm that learning outcomes are being met.

Using the Charting Student Progress Guide

The Charting Student Progress Guide is an effective tool in providing student feedback. Essentially it provides

- guidance in identifying learning experiences for the plan of learning
- guidance for student, educator and mentor in monitoring and evaluating students' progress over the cycle of the work-based learning experience
- evaluation of both generic attributes and professional skills
- opportunities for student, educator, and mentor to reflect upon personal and professional development
- structure for formal feedback sessions
- documents for educators' formal assessment

The Charting Student Progress Guide features a series of tables that cover two specific areas of learning outcomes. The first is "generic" outcomes or desirable attributes of a wide range of professional careers. The second is "professional" outcomes which relate directly to the particular course of study. An example is provided in part II. The listing of learning outcomes should not be viewed as prescriptive as all aspects will not be appropriate for each student or each particular workplace. Neither should an attempt be made to award a grade. Student development can be reflected by placing a tick in the box alongside each criterion that best reflects the student's level of development in that area. These criteria reflect levels of development from, for example, "lacks theoretical understanding and application skills"—to "demonstrates exemplary knowledge and skills."

The Charting Student Progress Guide should be completed at the end of the first block of time, midway through the work experience, then at its conclusion. This will provide a very comprehensive picture for educators, mentors, and the students themselves. Although intended to be qualitative rather than quantitative, it serves as one of the sources the educators can use for awarding a final grade at the end of the work experience.

The Charting Student Progress Guide can be used in a number of ways. It can be used independently by the student for self-assessment, then compared with the Guide completed by the mentor. Another strategy is for student and mentor to work through the Guide together. This provides an important way to develop trust and confidence in the mentoring relationship as each seeks ways to enhance personal and professional development. The discussion could reveal areas where students might improve, gaps in the students' knowledge and skills, and areas that require additional training to advance the level of strength represented. The Guide itself facilitates constructive criticism, an area which is invariably difficult for the mentor to provide and the student to receive in a positive manner. The Charting Student Progress Guide may also be a useful discussion point between educator and student or educator and mentor. Ultimately, it satisfies the need for an assessment of the student's development overall.

Gaining Mentors' Overall Perspective of Students' Learning

At the conclusion of the work-based learning experience, the educator should contact the mentor and discuss the student's development over the period. It is helpful to have a series of questions, distributed beforehand to the mentor, to guide this discussion. Such questions are also valuable because they

- guide the educators in the important process of evaluation
- create a consistent method of evaluation for the work-based experience
- ensure adequate and comparable information is gathered
- ensure students are treated equitably
- ensure evaluation methods are documented as normal academic practice

Evaluating the Students' Work-Based Learning Experience

Guiding Questions for the Mentor to Consider

At the conclusion of the work-based learning experience, a discussion should be held between the mentor and educator. The following questions have proved useful in gaining an overview of the students' growth and development.

1. Did the students participate willingly and fully in the experiences designed for them?

2. Did the students participate in scheduled consultations and demonstrate a positive attitude towards these?

3. Did the students show evidence of reflecting upon their learning?

4. Did the students make an effort to enhance their learning where gaps could be identified?

5. Did the students show interest in problems and issues in the workplace?

6. Where there was an opportunity, did the students apply problem-solving skills to such problems and issues?

7. Did the students demonstrate effective communication skills in the workplace?

8. Did the students at all times display professional behavior, such as respecting confidentiality and privacy, having respect for others, exhibiting punctuality, reliability, cooperativeness, and standards of dress and behavior in keeping with the organisation?

9. Did the students achieve the learning outcomes outlined in their plans of learning experiences? If not, why not?

10. How would you sum up the students' potential as emerging entry-level professionals?

Gathering Assessable Material for the Educators Forum

The work-based learning model advocates gathering a wide range of materials to assist in a multifaceted evaluation of the student's development during and after the work-based learning experience. This chapter has discussed the wide range of activities and materials collected. All these materials can then be used by the educators to finalize subject requirements. To gain that multifaceted view of the student's achievements, the following aspects should be considered:

- mentor's comments on overall performance at the conclusion of the work-based learning experience
- student's development as outlined in the Educating Student's Guide
- student's record of attendance at the workplace
- student's portfolio of achievements and commentary on these
- student's self assessment of learning and personal reflection upon goals, achievements, and future plans
- student's self assessment of achievements in the work-based experience
- educator's assessment of reflective learning during student seminars

The collaborative nature of the work-based learning model is also reflected in the formal assessment of students by the educators. An Educators Forum, comprising the academics involved in the work-based experience, is an efficient and effective way to bring together and consider all collected material and simultaneously to consider the functioning of the program. The work-based learning model recommends using the usual tertiary assessment for subjects completed as part of professional course requirements. A brief discussion of the rationale for assessment using the full range of available marks follows.

Rationale for Assessing Work-Based Learning Experiences

Assessing work-based learning experiences is often treated differently from other forms of assessment. Institutions differ on whether such work experience should be voluntary or required, whether such experience should be assessed solely as pass or fail, or whether the full range of marks awarded to other university subjects should be used. There are a number of reasons why students should be assessed using a full range of marks. The full range:

- reflects different levels of achievement
- signals the importance of the experience in the academic career
- motivates and guides the student's expectations
- contributes to an overview of the student's achievements
- adds to the overall record of the student's achievements for consideration of future study and scholarship potential

A decision to assess students using the full range of marks carries certain responsibilities. These include producing a subject guide, which details learning outcomes, subject requirements, assessment criteria, and assessment procedures.

Evaluating the Work-Based Learning Model

Evaluating the Work-Based Learning Model through Group Processes

There is a logical way to gain continuing feedback and evaluate synergies between the worlds of the student's personal and professional knowledge, tertiary professional education, and work-based learning experiences. In that introductory year of implementing the work-based learning model, a steering committee should be established with members chosen to represent the students, educators, and mentors. Meetings of the steering committee should coincide with milestones in the development of the work-based learning model. The following milestones are suggested:

- after the initial predetermined block of students' work-based learning
- midway through the cycle
- at the conclusion of the cycle

This steering committee may be raising difficult issues for consideration and resolution, and the selection of the chair of this committee is an important decision. Ideally, the chair should be outside the group of students, educators, and mentors in the work-based learning program. The chair should understand the principles of adult learning, experiential learning, and professional education. Such a person is positioned to identify the important issues from the particular instances, to offer strategies outside the professional experience of those on the committee, and to facilitate discussion and resolution should differences of opinion arise.

Evaluating the Work-Based Learning Model through Individual Views

While the steering committee provides representative views during and after the work-based learning model's first full cycle, it is also important to seek the views of individual students and mentors. At the conclusion of the cycle, a questionnaire, individually tailored to student or mentor, can be distributed for anonymous feedback. Such a questionnaire can provide evaluative comments on

- workshops provided and needed
- organizational aspects
- communication between educator, student, and mentor
- design and use of the plan of learning
- students' and mentors' performance—expectations and possibilities
- students' professional knowledge—basic and desirable
- educators' and mentors' strategies for enhancing student learning
- educators' printed materials
- strengths and weaknesses and suggestions for improvements

These individual evaluations, when consolidated, provide an overview of how well the work-based learning model is working. These written materials can then be considered in conjunction with the expressed views of the steering committee. The resulting information forms the basis for a plan to implement changes and create enhancements to the work-based learning model.

The next chapter details the practical application of the model.

6

Practical Application of the Model

Introduction

Preparation is one of the important keys to the success of the model. Educator, mentor, and student all need to have the same vision of the process and the anticipated outcomes. It is the responsibility of the educator to see that this is achieved.

Gaining Support for the Program

Where work-based learning programs within professional education are a new venture, it would be strategic to bring together key employers in the professional community and opinion leaders in the community's professional association. The main objectives would be to explain and gain support for the concept and to clarify issues such as

- purpose and short- and long-term goals
- benefits to the students, mentors, organizations, and the profession
- roles and responsibilities of mentors, educators, and students
- interaction between mentors, educators, and students
- community support and training

It should also be recognized that not all professions have a culture that supports this level of commitment to the educational process of its new graduates. One way to overcome this drawback and gain the necessary support is to target key members of the profession who are in positions of influence. If these people can be persuaded of the overall benefits of the work-based learning model they may help to promote it more generally. Or, at the very least, their endorsement may influence others.

Criteria and a Process for the Selection of the Students

The criteria and process for selecting students will vary from course to course and institution to institution. In some cases, experiential learning is a required component of academic study and in others it is optional. However, there are some factors that contribute to the success of an experiential learning program.

One is the location of the program in the structure of the degree. To gain maximum benefit, students need to have completed core professional studies. This means they will be able to work with some level of competence within the workplace. It also means that they will have a body of theory to apply in the workplace, enabling them to integrate theory and practice.

Much of the potential value of the work-based learning model is a result of the students becoming a part of the workplace team. From experience it seems that a full two-week block of time is sufficient for students to be socialized into their organizations.

It also may be necessary to consider an exemption where students can make a case for recognition of prior learning if they are currently employed and performing professional tasks. However, the important issue to consider is the nature of the tasks performed. Because students are working does not necessarily mean they are performing professional duties.

Criteria and a Process for Selecting Mentors and Matching Mentors and Students

The selection of mentors is controlled by many factors, and the final decision is often based on a judgment that is founded on experience. Underpinning the process are strong links between the educators and their professional community. These links must be built on mutual trust and respect. Mentors need to have the same vision for the outcomes of the work experience and be willing to make the required commitment to the program and to the student. Although there seems little evidence, other than anecdotal, it appears that this type of commitment can be obtained more easily in the professions that are built on a service ethic. In our own profession of librarianship, for example, there is a very strong willingness on the part of the professional community to contribute in this way to the education of future professionals.

However, more practically, when educators consider the knowledge, skills, and professional attitudes that the students have and those they want to develop, they can begin to identify suitable mentors. This process is based on their own knowledge of the possible pool of mentors and their organizations or on recommendations from trusted professional colleagues. The process can be time consuming because there are often factors that preclude a possible mentor, even a willing one. For example, where an organization is experiencing a period of instability, such as a restructure, it is usually not appropriate to place a student in the situation at that time. Sometimes even mentors who are committed may feel that they need a break after having mentored a student, or several students, in the past.

Another issue that impacts the process is the educator's knowledge of the students themselves, including the students' demonstrated attitude to work and their level of achievement. Sometimes even knowledge of the student's personality might affect the decision of whom to select as a mentor.

Although students' opinions about the type of organization in which they would like to work are considered, they should not be placed in organizations where they know the mentor. Such a situation may compromise the mentor's ability to give constructive feedback.

Developing the Shared Vision (Training)

The success of this work-based learning model lies largely in the synergy created by the interaction of the three worlds. For this to occur, each person must have the same vision of the program and the expected outcomes. The responsibility for developing this lies with the educators and it is facilitated through workshops for both students and mentors.

Designing and Delivering Workshops for Mentors

An important part of the workshop for the mentors is helping them understand their role in the learning experiences of the students. Although they are experienced practitioners, they may have difficulty converting "what they do" into a developmental learning experience for someone who is only partway through their professional education. However, mentors usually find this part of the process quite valuable. It forces them to reflect on their own work practices, question them, and sometimes even refine them.

A typical mentor training workshop should include sessions on

- socializing the students into the workplace team
- developing a plan of learning
- giving feedback
- using reflective learning and problem solving

Socializing the Students into the Workplace Team

The purpose of commencing a learning experience of this type with the student spending a solid block of time, for example two weeks, is to provide opportunity for them to become part of the workplace team. The mentor can assist this process by

- introducing the student to all members of the immediate work area
- introducing the student to all members of work areas with whom the student will interact
- allowing the student to participate in organizational induction programs
- ensuring the student understands workplace social conventions. This includes simple customs such as whether they need to bring their own mug for morning tea and whether they should contribute to the cost of the tea/coffee, etc.
- providing relevant background material for the student to read such as annual reports
- ensuring that the student has a place to work and everything that might be necessary to perform the tasks they are required to complete

Developing a Plan of Learning

The individualized plans of learning are critical to the success of the learning experience as they embody the negotiated agreements between the mentors and the students. After examining the students' CVs and meeting with them to discuss the work experience, the mentors design a draft plan of learning that is then discussed with the students. When both mentor and student feel the plan meets the needs of the student, it is then submitted to the educator for approval. The plans are based on the students' personal and professional goals; the knowledge, skills, and attributes that they already possess; and the ones they want to develop—within the constraints of what the organization can offer. The plans are not formal contracts but developmental guides which can be modified, if necessary, over the period of the work experience.

To develop the plans, mentors must translate the work tasks into incremental learning steps so that by the end of the work experience, students have experienced all appropriate aspects of the workplace activities. To achieve this mentors should focus on the tasks that collectively represent their job and then answer the following questions:

- What is the focus of my work area?
- What aspects of this work would I like the student to learn?
- What tasks should I provide so the student can learn about this?
- How will I provide feedback to the student?

The number of aspects selected will depend on the nature of the work, the length of the learning experience, and the students' knowledge, skills, and attributes. Having identified perhaps four aspects of their work, the mentors then identify the incremental learning steps that they need to design so that the students learn to perform the various aspects of their work at a professional level. For each aspect of the work, depending on what it is, mentors might need to design a process involving four or five learning activities that extend over a number of weeks.

The completed plans are then sent to the educators for approval. Having regard for the individual student, mentor, and organization, the educator ensures that the

- plan contains achievable learning outcomes
- scope of the experience is sufficiently broad to understand the work area
- activities and tasks are appropriate to achieving the learning outcomes
- supervision and mentoring provisions are appropriate

Since the plan is a developmental guide to learning, changes may be necessary. Student and mentor may overestimate or underestimate abilities and the time required to develop or enhance knowledge and skills. The mentoring relationship as it develops may undergo changes and different opportunities may become available. Given the collaborative nature of the learning plan, proposed changes should involve all those who participated in its development.

Once the plan is finalized, a range of opportunities exists to make connections between the three worlds. Student, educator, and mentor work collaboratively to make these links. An example of a plan of learning is included in part II.

Giving Feedback

Ongoing constructive feedback plays an important part in the developmental learning process of the students. Mentors need to understand that there are different types of feedback and the value of each type to the students.

Immediate feedback can occur on the spot and is usually informal in nature. It can be solicited by the students as they deal with uncertainty or given unsolicited by the mentors. Unsolicited positive feedback of this type is very reassuring for students and assists them in developing self-confidence. Where necessary, negative feedback, as long as it is constructive in nature, is more easily handled by students if offered at the point at which the problem occurs. If ignored, small problems can easily develop into larger ones.

Formal feedback sessions are also important, and the timing of these should be designated at the commencement of the learning experience. These sessions need only be short, but they should be regular. The sessions should be used to review progress in terms of the plan of learning, which can then be adjusted if necessary.

The Charting Student Progress Guide can also be used as an effective tool in the feedback process. The primary function of the Charting Student Progress Guide is to record the student's development over the period of the work experience. This is achieved as the mentor and the student reflect on and discuss the student's performance against the criteria listed in the guide. Mentors' comments and feedback are integral to the process.

Using Reflective Learning and Problem Solving

This model of learning follows the Socratic method. Mentors need to understand that an important part of their role is to encourage the student to question, to reflect, and, even at times, to take risks. As noted, the process of reflecting can occur in a formal situation when mentors and students are discussing the Charting Student Progress

Guide. However, mentors should also plan strategies that will push students' boundaries to the extent that enhanced learning will occur. They should provide opportunities for students to have some autonomy knowing that they are there, in the background, if the student falters. Some mentors have reported that they have deliberately allowed a student to make a mistake if they thought that was the best way to achieve a certain learning outcome. This is an example of both challenging and supporting the student.

Mentors also participate in their own reflective processes. Such processes examine their own workplace practices, the best way to translate them into learning experiences for the students, as well as student learning and development. Sometimes this process causes a mentor to change a workplace practice. In the normal working life of a busy professional, time for reflection is often overlooked.

At the end of the program mentors must also reflect on the total work experience when they are asked to evaluate the student. Although it is the educators' responsibility for awarding the final grade, mentors' views are extremely important as they are the ones who have worked closely with the students over the full period of the work experience.

It has been found that during the workshops new mentors find it useful to listen to previous mentors and students talk about the experience. Because it is usually a positive experience, it is reassuring for those undertaking it for the first time to have questions answered by this group. Likewise, students who have completed the program value the contribution their mentors have made to their own learning and personal and professional development. This student view of the mentor's role is also encouraging for new mentors. Mentors also find it useful to have a description of the course the students are undertaking, particularly the description, and learning outcomes of the subjects the students have already completed.

Designing and Delivering Workshops for Students

Student preparation should commence the teaching term before the work experience itself. The preparation is best offered through a workshop where students

- identify personal goals
- analyze the knowledge, skills, and professional attitudes they already possess

- identify the knowledge, skills, and professional attitudes they would like to develop
- learn how to write CVs
- learn strategies for taking control of their own learning
- gain a greater understanding of their professional responsibilities while on the work experience program

Because younger students in particular often find it difficult to analyze the knowledge, skills, and professional attitudes they already possess and identify those they would like to develop, the process usually needs to be facilitated. However, this is an important step for a number of reasons, because it

- provides a benchmark against which future learning can be compared
- encourages students when they reflect, both during the work experience and at its conclusion, to "see" the growth that has occurred
- assists mentors as they plan the work experience from the organization's point of view
- provides a reference point for the educators, as they encourage students in the process of self-reflection

The process of identifying the knowledge, skills, and attitudes students would like to develop through the work experience assists educators when selecting the placement. It is also important for the mentors as it helps them design students' plans of learning. As students should have completed their core professional studies before beginning their work experience, they usually have an understanding of their profession, its various facets, and the opportunities for specialization that are available within the particular profession.

The book and video set, *Possibilities and Probabilities*, provides suitable preparatory material to use in workshop situations with the students (Alderman and Milne, assisted by Gemmell 1997). Student modules from this kit are provided in part II. They address

- analyzing existing personal, technical, and professional skills
- identifying desired personal, technical, and professional skills
- setting the framework for the learning experience
- understanding the workplace culture

- handling conflict in the workplace
- managing time
- accepting and reflecting on constructive feedback

The video, which is set in the workplace, is useful as a basis for discussion to give a sense of reality to the anticipated learning experience. It features students, filmed on location, talking about their work experiences. In a variety of organizations, students talk about making the most of the opportunity, accepting the responsibility for the outcomes of the work experience, and, particularly, what they might have done differently a second time around. The mentors talk about the importance of students taking control of their own learning, saying what it is they want to learn and setting their own professional goals.

Maintaining Communication between Student, Educator, and Mentor

Maintaining open and continuing communication between student, educator, and mentor is essential to ensure all is proceeding well. Individual communication is greatly facilitated by e-mail, facsimile, and the telephone. Opportunities for group consideration of issues include newsletters, either paper or electronic. An electronic bulletin board can facilitate exchange of views, offer support and advice, and develop a sense of community.

Each method has advantages and disadvantages. Communication via newsletter or electronic bulletin board adds another element to the educators' already large role in facilitating the model. Yet such communication may enable ideas and issues to be shared that might not otherwise be introduced through the individual contact, educator's visits, or student seminars. Invariably all those involved in work-based learning experiences are busy people, and it is important to establish and maintain communication strategies that are deemed essential for the effective operation of the model.

Designing Documentation

It is recommended that a number of documents support a learning experience of this type. As a supplement to the training workshops and to provide a ready-reference source of information about the program, mentors and students both benefit from having guidelines, requirements, and procedures formally stated. Developing the written material also assists educators clarify their own ideas and thinking. Documentation should include:

- handbook
- Charting Student Progress Guide
- subject guide

The Handbook

The handbook should include all of the information that underpins the program. It becomes a primary tool for all participants as it will promote their continued understanding of a shared vision. A copy should be given to all mentors and students at the workshops. It is also a useful document to give to potential mentors as they consider the possibility of their involvement. The handbook should contain

- a brief rationale for the program
- a description of the benefits to students, mentors, the organization, and the profession
- the responsibilities of the students, mentors, and educators
- a statement about the requirements of the plan of learning
- administrative details

The Charting Student Progress Guide

The basic premise behind this model is that complementing professional studies with work-based learning experiences, with consideration of the student's personal and professional development, produces enhanced learning outcomes. The mentor in the workplace plays an essential role in "educating" the learner, and that process is formally outlined in the plan of learning. But equally important is a means of evaluating the student's development as the experience progresses. The Charting Student Progress Guide is a means of charting this development.

The Subject Guide

The subject guide is for the students and it should include all of the items officially required by the university for such documents. In addition, it needs to include specific information related to work experience programs such as information about insurance and workers compensation.

Other information should relate to the specific work experience subject and include:

- learning outcomes
- reflective learning guidelines
- details of the preparatory workshops
- assessment requirements
- required texts
- enrolment and progression information

Commitment Required

There is no doubt that implementing the work-based learning model involves a significant time commitment on the part of the educator, mentor, and student. However, based on our ten years' experience developing, refining, and formally evaluating the work-based learning model, it is clear that the benefits for all involved far outweigh the time commitment required. Anecdotal evidence from employers about these new graduates suggests that they have made the transition from study to work with exceptional entry-level knowledge, skills, and professional attitudes. Mentors and students have attested to a high level of personal and professional benefits for themselves. Where there is cohesion among a professional community, its members value having input into the educational process of its new graduates.

7

Conclusion

The work-based learning model features a collaborative teaching, student-centered approach. Expert practitioners work with educators and students to design individual plans of learning for students. These are based on the knowledge, skills, and professional attitudes the students already possess and what the organization can offer, and they provide for the development of those areas the students have identified as important to their professional course and to themselves personally.

One of the key critical success factors of the model is the use it makes of facilitated mentoring. By "elevating" the workplace supervisor to the role of mentor, a new dimension is added to the relationship this person shares with the student. It is a relationship where the mentor recognizes the student as an emerging professional. In so doing, the mentor accepts the responsibility for assisting the student, not only to develop practical workplace skills, but also to make the transition from student to new professional. The mentor, with the educator, creates a context for the student's learning experience and facilitates the learning through a variety of processes.

The mentoring relationship is based on Margo Murray's (1991) model of facilitated mentoring where there is a deliberate pairing of a more skilled or experienced person with a lesser skilled or experienced one, with the agreed upon goal of having the lesser skilled person grow and develop. Facilitated mentoring provides a structure and a series of processes that guide the desired behavior changes. In this instance these include the professional learning and personal growth of the student. The model described also draws heavily on the theory and application of experiential learning as proposed by writers such as Kolb (1984) and Mezirow and associates (1990). Key elements of these theories are that the nature of learning is highly individual, dependent on the way we construct meaning from our experiences (Mezirow and associates 1990), and involves a process whereby knowledge is created through the transformation of experience (Kolb 1984). These elements have influenced both the design of the model and its application.

The actual process of turning experience into learning is facilitated through the adoption of Boud's (1993) "model of learning from experience" (38). In his model, Boud outlines three stages: preparation, experience, and reflective processes. The preparation stage considers the learner's background experiences, what the learning experience itself offers, and the knowledge and skills the learner brings to the experience. During the experience, the learner interacts with all aspects of the organization and learns by observing, participating, intervening, and influencing what is taking place. The reflective processes cause the learner to return to the experience, recall feelings, and reevaluate the experience.

Writers agree that reflecting on learning experiences does not come naturally or intuitively for many people, but that the process can be facilitated (Clifford 1999; Douchy, Segers, and Sluijsman 1999; Birenbaum and Douchy 1996; Griffee 1995; Boud and Knights 1994; Johns 1994; Boud and Falchikov 1989). Boud (1985) suggests that educators provide a context and space to learn, give support and encouragement, listen to the student, and provide access to particular devices which may be of use. The work-based learning model introduces the mentor as a key person, to work in tandem with the educator, in this type of learning experience. This work-based learning model assumes that the student's most effective work-based learning will take place at the intersection of three "worlds." Connections between the worlds are facilitated by collaborative processes between the educator and mentor who develop strategies to encourage the practice of reflective learning.

Personal strategies for the students include recording and reflecting in journals, providing evidence of learning through portfolios, and examining learning through self-assessment. Group-based strategies include case studies, role plays, and problem-based learning. The aim of all these strategies is to enhance student learning through work-based experience by bringing together the three worlds of student experience, tertiary professional education, and work-based learning. The point where the three worlds intersect embodies the practical application of the underpinning theory and is enhanced by elevating the role of the workplace supervisor to that of mentor.

The development of the shared vision, essential for the success of the program and ultimately for achieving the desired learning outcomes for the student, is facilitated by the educators. Such a vision is achieved by providing workshop sessions for both students and mentors. Students need to take control of their own learning. To be able to do this, they first need to recognize the knowledge, skills, and professional attitudes they already possess and those they want to develop. Like the process of reflective learning, this is not something they find easy to do, but it can be facilitated through a structured process.

Materials such as the kit *Probabilities and Possibilities* (Alderman and Milne, assisted by Gemmell 1997) provide useful content for workshop sessions with the students. The workshops for mentors should help them understand their role in the learning experiences of the students. This includes developing the plan of learning, giving feedback, and playing an active role in encouraging the students to question, to reflect, and, where appropriate, to take risks. The individualized plans of learning are critical to the success of the learning experience as they embody the negotiated agreement between the mentors and the students. Having a level of flexibility means that the plans can be revised to accommodate unforeseen opportunities or a variation in the anticipated rate or level of student learning.

Maintaining open communication between student, educator, and mentor is also an important feature for the success of the model. Once the program has begun, and after the educator's visit to the organization, mentors and students work together in the organization without any direct input from the educator. However, each needs to be aware that the educator is available, if and when required, for consultation and advice.

A number of documents support a learning experience of this type. These should include a handbook that will act as a reference tool for all participants and help to maintain the shared vision as well as a subject guide for students. In addition, a document to record and reflect student development over the period of the work experience should be developed. Such a document can be used by the mentor when giving feedback to the student.

The practical application of the work-based learning model is multifaceted and requires a high level of commitment from educators, students, and mentors. The adequate preparation of students and mentors is essential. However, once the facilitating processes have been established, each mentoring relationship takes on a life of its own. Motivation for mentors is maintained through the intrinsic benefits that the program offers them. Through the relationship with their mentors, students quickly become a part of the organizational team. They feel valued, and this increases their level of self-confidence. In responding to the challenges provided by their mentors they extend the boundaries of what they believed they were capable of achieving. The ability to reflect on their experiences is encouraged by their mentors and honed through the workshops and seminars run by the educators.

As an example of work-based learning within a professional course of study, the work-based learning model offers enhanced learning opportunities to the students and intrinsic and practical advantages to the mentors, to participating organizations, and ultimately to the profession. Students from the program who have now been in the workforce for several years testify that the level of self-confidence they developed as a result of their participation gave them a market edge when they faced their first job interview. This enabled them to make the transition from university to workplace far more easily and effectively.

Part II

8

Supplementary Material

Introduction

Part II contains a range of activities that can be used by educators during all aspects of the work experience, from preparing students and mentors through to assisting students moving into the professional workforce. It also includes some examples of the documents used to support the model and referred to in part I.

Ideally, the activities for students should be used with educators and students working together, as the educators are the catalysts for developing the students' ability for personal reflection that is a critical aspect of the model. While the activities can be used by the students working independently, experience has shown that this is less effective because the ability to reflect on personal attributes or past experience is not a natural ability, but one that needs to be developed and then fostered.

The supplementary material provided in part II has been developed and refined over a period of ten years of the authors working with the model. It should be used with reference to table 1.1 that gives an overview and linear representation of the model. The supplementary material is grouped into two sections:

1. Set of 20 modules to be used with students. Table 2.1 provides an overview of the modules including the key concept and anticipated learning outcomes for each. Modules 1 through 14 relate to the three phases of the model: the preparation phase, the experience phase, and the evaluation phase. Modules 15 through 20 include some additional activities to assist students as they apply for their first professional position. At the end of this section are further checklists, guidelines, and samples.

2. Sample of documents referred to in part I. The University of Canberra subject based on this model is called Partners in Learning and is generally known at the university and in the

profession as PAL. The examples of documents provided in this section are those used for PAL students and mentors. The documents include

- Student Expression of Interest Form
- developing the plan of learning experience
- plan of learning
- handbook
- Charting Student Progress Guide
- journal

Overview of Student Modules

Table 2.1 Student Modules

Module	Module Title	Learning Outcomes
1	Analyzing Your Personal Skills	**Key concept** *developing the ability to analyze your personal skills* **Learning outcomes** On completing this module you will have: • *identified the knowledge and skills of professional practice* • *analyzed your personal skills* • *identified areas where personal skill development is required*
2	Analyzing Your Technical Skills	**Key concept** *developing the ability to analyze your technical skills* **Learning outcomes** On completing this module you will have: • *analyzed your technical skills* • *identified areas where technical skill development is required*

Module	Module Title	Learning Outcomes
3	Analyzing Your Professional Skills	**Key concept** *developing the ability to analyze your professional skills* **Learning outcomes** On completing this module you will have: • *analyzed your professional skills* • *identified areas where professional skill development is required*
4	Finding Out about the Workplace	**Key concept** *gaining an understanding of the workplace* **Learning outcomes** On completing this module you will have: • *gained an understanding of the mission and strategic plans of the organization* • *be able to evaluate the messages communicated by the organization* • *understand the organizational structure*
5	Managing Your Time	**Key concept** *juggling study and work experience* **Learning outcomes** On completing this module you will understand how to: • *prioritize your commitments* • *manage your time effectively*
6	Developing Professional Attributes	**Key concept** *identifying and understanding those attributes which are the hallmarks of being a professional in your area* **Learning outcomes** On completing this module you will have: • *identified attributes of professionalism* • *internalized professional attributes*

Module	Module Title	Learning Outcomes
7	Setting the Framework for Your Learning Experiences	**Key concept** *developing a shared view of the workplace experience* **Learning outcomes** On completing this module you will have: • *considered expectations and responsibilities of student and supervisor* • *negotiated learning opportunities*
8	Evaluating Organizational Culture	**Key concept** *identifying elements of organizational culture* **Learning outcomes** On completing this module you will have: • *gained an understanding of workplace culture* • *identified aspects that contribute to or detract from the effective management of organizational culture* • *identified models of effectively managing organizational culture*
9	Communicating with Your Workplace Supervisor	**Key concept** *maximizing communication opportunities* **Learning outcomes** On completing this module you will have considered the importance of: • *planning opportunities for communication* • *seizing opportunities for communication* • *developing effective communication*

Module	Module Title	Learning Outcomes
10	Learning from Your Workplace Supervisor	**Key concept** *identifying strategies for learning from the workplace supervisor* **Learning outcomes** On completing this module you will be able to: • *identify opportunities for learning* • *plan learning experiences* • *reflect on learning experiences*
11	Dealing with Conflict in the Workplace	**Key concept** *understanding the nature of conflict and developing strategies for its resolution* **Learning outcomes** On completing this module you will be able to: • *clarify conflict* • *identify strategies for managing conflict* • *prevent conflict*
12	Using Problem-Based Learning	**Key concept** *developing problem-solving strategies for the workplace* **Learning outcomes** On completing this module you will have: • *researched and analyzed problems in professional practice* • *developed effective solutions to problems* • *managed group processes for effective results*

Module	Module Title	Learning Outcomes
13	Accepting and Reflecting on Constructive Feedback	**Key concept** *valuing feedback as a tool in the learning process* **Learning outcomes** On completing this module you will understand the importance of: • *accepting and managing constructive feedback*
14	Reflecting on Your Work Experience or Internship	**Key concept** *evaluating your work experience or internship* **Learning outcomes** On completing this module you will be able to: • *identify areas of learning and personal growth* • *evaluate the degree of learning and personal growth* • *evaluate the reasons for learning goals not met*
15	Matching the Job with Your Skills	**Key concept** *locating information about jobs and understanding advertisements* **Learning outcomes** On completing this module you will be able to: • *identify information sources about jobs* • *match your skills to job advertisements*
16	Creating Resumes	**Key concept** *understanding the resume as a marketing and communication tool* **Learning outcomes** On completing this module you will be able to: • *write a resume which communicates*

Module	Module Title	Learning Outcomes
17	Applying for Your First Position	**Key concept** *writing the best possible job application* **Learning outcomes** On completing this module you will be able to: • *address the selection criteria*
18	Understanding the Basics of Cover Letters	**Key concept** *understanding the key features of cover letters* **Learning outcomes** On completing this module you will be able to: • *identify the key elements of cover letters* • *create appropriately styled cover letters*
19	Creating Cover Letters	**Key concept** *marketing yourself through a letter of introduction* **Learning outcomes** On completing this module you will be able to: • *analyze the requirements of effective letters of introduction* • *select an appropriate style for your letter*
20	Making the Most of Your Job Interview	**Key concept** *achieving a successful interview* **Learning outcomes** On completing this module you will be able to: • *find out about the organization/position* • *develop an interview strategy* • *achieve a strong interview performance*

Module 1: Analyzing Your Personal Skills

Key concept

developing the ability to analyze your personal skills

Learning outcomes

On completing this module you will have:

- *identified the knowledge and skills of professional practice*
- *analyzed your personal skills*
- *identified areas where personal skill development is required*

What are the Knowledge and Skills of Professional Practice?

In everything we do, we use our knowledge and skills. When we are thinking about the areas of professional practice we will work in, there are three types of skills we will be using. These are broad-base or personal skills, work-related or professional skills, and job-specific or technical skills.

People usually find it easy to talk about their technical skills and to assess how well they can apply them. However, this is not all there is to being successful in your chosen field. What you can do (technical skills) has to be put alongside what you know (professional skills) and how well you can get things done (personal skills). It is your ability to use all three kinds of skills that counts.

Personal Skills

Personal skills are often called "transferable" skills because they can be used in a variety of settings and it is generally considered that these skills are crucial in the development of a competent professional. It may be comforting for you to know that employers are not just concerned with subjects and marks. They hire people, not just pieces of paper with "degree" stamped on them. They look for people with potential, who are flexible and can learn, and who can transfer the skills they have developed in one area of their life and use them in another. All graduates, whatever their discipline, have had training in collecting, analyzing, and presenting information, to learn to get along with people of all kinds, and to acquire a general knowledge of what is going along in the world. These skills are marketable and include an ability to

- demonstrate interpersonal skills
- solve problems
- demonstrate organizing ability
- demonstrate self-motivation
- think independently
- show initiative
- show diligence
- achieve objectives
- demonstrate self-confidence
- manage information
- show energy and enthusiasm
- assess and judge issues
- grasp abstract ideas
- manage time
- show flexibility
- handle conflict
- accept responsibility
- show leadership
- show imagination
- act competitively
- show analytical skills
- communicate effectively

Task 1: Analyzing Your Personal Skills

This section sets out some personal skills which have been shown to be important in identifying competent professionals, the kind of person who is likely to be hired, and the kind of person colleagues respect.

A brief definition is given of each skill as well as some examples of how you may have used each skill in everyday life. In the space provided under each, write down some examples of where, in your studies or through work or life experiences, you have shown that you have these skills.

Skill: Works to Set Standards

This can involve following set procedures or attending to detail; in these cases, there are agreed outputs.

Examples: organizing a function, building a model, keeping a laboratory workbook.

Examples of this skill gained through my course or previous work experience include:

Skill: Communicates Well with People

This involves being a good listener, as well as getting your point across orally and in writing by expressing yourself clearly, explaining things to people, thinking "on your feet," and presenting a clear case.

You do this when you teach someone, write a letter to the newspaper, give a seminar, or listen to someone's problems without interrupting.

Examples of this skill gained through my course or previous work experience include:

Skill: Sets and Achieves Goals

This involves many sub-skills and includes the ability to analyze a complex task into its component parts, to manage the necessary resources (people, money, and equipment), and to envisage an outcome. We often refer to this skill as the ability to manage. Time management and stress management are among the more important aspects of these skills. You set and achieve goals when you are involved in a club or society, chair a meeting or committee, study independently. Being able to manage your time means being able to identify your priorities and meet deadlines. Perhaps you manage stress through exercise, relaxation, or some quite different kind of activity.

Examples of this skill gained through my course or previous work experience include:

Skill: Shows Initiative

This involves being able to see other ways of doing things, seizing opportunities, taking the initiative.

You do this, for example, when you strike up conversations with strangers, or when you volunteer an idea, or when you design an innovative way of doing something.

Examples of this skill gained through my course or previous work experience include:

_____

_____

Skill: Responds to Needs

This involves being able to modify what you are doing to suit someone else and assumes that your people skills are good enough to enable you to observe or identify what the other person's needs are.

Examples of this skill gained through my course or previous work experience include:

_____

_____

Skill: Demonstrates Leadership

What is your leadership potential? Leadership is making maximum use of people and resources within a group to help the group achieve its objectives. Any job which involves directing a team, managing a project, supervising people, or teaching a skill is essentially about leadership.

Examples of this skill gained through my course or previous work experience include:

_____

_____

Skill: Shows Enthusiasm and Energy

This involves eagerness and a strong interest in something.
Eagerness is often demonstrated through nonverbal behavior, such as speed of speech and tone of voice. Enthusiasm can be shown, for example, through active participation in a club or society or through involvement in some event or activity.

Examples of this skill gained through my course or previous work experience include:

_____

_____

Skill: **Works Well with Others**

This involves being team-oriented rather than egocentric; being supportive of superiors or subordinates in an organization, club, or society; recognizing people's strengths.

You show this, for example, when you are part of a sports team or through voluntary work or through group study projects, especially undertaking fieldwork.

Examples of this skill gained through my course or previous work experience include:

_____

_____

Skill: **Shows Resourcefulness**

This involves having imagination and being able to improvise, being willing to try new ideas or adapt old ones, looking to the future and identifying what will be out of date before this is generally recognized.

Resourceful people can usually offer a solution to a problem; they have schemes that work; they deal with ideas, or can see the possibilities in applying an idea.

Examples of this skill gained through my course or previous work experience include:

_____

_____

Skill: **Takes Risks**

This involves gathering information to narrow the gap between the known and the unknown and acting or taking a decision based on what might be expected to happen, rather than on previous experience.

To a greater or lesser extent you do this whenever you do something you have not done before and you find the potential outcome uncertain or unsettling.

Examples of this skill gained through my course or previous work experience include:

_____

_____

Task 2: Identifying Other Personal Skills Relating to Your Profession

What are the other personal skills you possess which you feel are important to your profession. You may wish to analyze these in the same way. Using the analysis of your personal skills, complete the section below to show which personal skills are important for the areas of professional practice in which you are interested and how you can show that you have those skills.

Personal Skill	Evidence/Experience

Task 3: Identifying Personal Skills That Need Developing

Briefly state the personal skills that you would like to develop through the work experience:

_____

_____

_____

_____

Module 2: Analyzing Your Technical Skills

Key concept

developing the ability to analyze your technical skills

Learning outcomes

On completing this module you will have:

* *analyzed your technical skills*
* *identified areas where technical skill development is required*

Technical Skills

Technical skills are the know-how of your particular area of professional practice and are the skills which relate to getting things done. Although they may involve the use of technology or equipment, this is not always the case. While some are common to jobs at certain levels in organizations, others are specific to a given kind of work or professional practice. Four common technical skills are:

* communication skills—written, oral, listening
* administrative skills
* computer skills
* analytical and research skills

Task 1: Identifying Technical Skills

In the tables below, some aspects of these technical skills are presented. Add any others which are important to the areas in which you are interested and delete any which do not apply. When you are satisfied that the list of common technical skills is complete, rate your competence on each, and where you think it appropriate, add a comment about your achievements using this skill.

Communication Skills

	Low	Medium	High
Public speaking			
Report writing			
Interviewing			

Comments

Administrative Skills

	Low	Medium	High
Allocating priorities			
Evaluating			
Budgeting			

Comments

Computer Skills

	Low	Medium	High
Keyboard skills			
Familiarity with general office software			
Familiarity with specialist software			

Comments

_____

_____

Analytical and Research Skills

	Low	Medium	High
Statistical analysis			
Information retrieval			

Comments

_____

_____

Task 2: Identifying Technical Skills That Need Developing

Briefly state the technical skills that you would like to develop through the work experience.

_____

_____

Module 3: Analyzing Your Professional Skills

Key concept

developing the ability to analyze your professional skills

Learning outcomes

On completing this module you will have:

- *analyzed your professional skills*
- *identified areas where professional skill development is required*

Professional Skills

These relate to your knowledge of the industry and of the theory, principles, and practice which guide the professional decisions you may have to make. Professional skills are sometimes difficult to identify for people new to a field of practice. However, if you have gathered information systematically about the professional area in which you are interested, then you will have made a good start. Useful sources of information about the professional skills of your chosen area include the accreditation requirements of the professional or industry association, course outlines for your program of study, and job advertisements.

Task 1: Analyze Your Knowledge of Your Profession

Knowledge of the industry or profession, its beliefs and attitudes, its standards and code of conduct, and the way its members make contact and exchange professional views are important elements of professional knowledge and skill which are all too often overlooked. These are introduced in the following table. Rate your knowledge by checking the appropriate box.

Knowledge of Your Profession

	Low	Medium	High
Knowledge of key professionals			
Understanding of professional values and beliefs			
Knowledge of current key issues			
Knowledge of professional association's activities (if applicable)			
Knowledge of professional journals and newsletters			
Knowledge of professional mentoring programs			

If you feel you are lacking in aspects of professional knowledge, identify some strategies you can implement immediately to begin to rectify this.

_____

_____

_____

Task 2: Identifying Professional Skills That Need Developing

Briefly state the professional skills that you would like to develop through the work experience.

_____

_____

_____

_____

Module 4: Finding Out about the Workplace

Key concept

gaining an understanding of the workplace

Learning outcome:

On completing this module you will:

- *have gained an understanding of the mission and stratgic plans of the organization*

- *be able to evaluate the messages communicated by the organization*

- *understand the organizational structure*

Task 1: Understanding the Organization's Mission

Acquire the organization's mission statement, strategic plan, or other statement about its goals.

a)   In your own words, state briefly what are the organization's main goals.

_____

_____

_____

_____

b)   What do you think are the two most important strategies used by the organization to move into the future?

_____

_____

_____

_____

Task 2: Communicating the Message

Select two documents from a range of information sources about the organization. These could include annual reports, brochures, posters, videos, web sites, etc.

a) What are the most important messages the organization is communicating about itself through these documents?

_____

_____

_____

_____

Task 3: Understanding the Organizational Structure

Acquire a description (possibly available as a diagram) of the organizational structure that includes job positions and responsibilities.

a) Identify the areas with which your section interacts.

_____

_____

_____

_____

b) Identify the work activities both internal and external in the organization relationships.

_____

_____

_____

_____

c) Briefly state how the areas in which you are based contribute to the larger organization.

_____

_____

_____

_____

Module 5: Managing Your Time

Key concept

juggling study and work experience

Learning outcomes

On completing this module you will understand how to:

* *prioritize your commitments*
* *manage your time effectively*

Task 1: Finding Out How You Use Your Time

Try keeping a diary for a couple of days, recording

* how you plan to use your time
* what happened in practice
* why there was a difference (assuming not everything went according to plan!)

Most people find they are surprised at how much time they waste. One of the secrets of being effective is to concentrate on doing things that really make a difference, ignoring those which are not particularly important or perhaps are not really necessary to do at all.

Task 2: Setting Your Priorities

a)   List all the items which you need to do in the next two days.

_____

_____

_____

b) Which ones are most important? Add dates for those which must
    be done by a particular time.

_____

_____

_____

A common trap is to put off lengthy tasks which do not have a
particular deadline, or which are not due for a long time, even though
they are very important!

Now, look again at your list in (a) above and number your tasks in
order of importance, taking into account when they are due but also
making sure you spend some time on the really important, long-term
ones. Then, start with task number 1!

Task 3: Organizing Yourself

There are some basic rules which should help you organize
yourself. Try to apply these rules for a couple of days and note whether
you have improved your organizing ability.

Rule 1: Put It in Writing

This is what you did in task 2: you made a "to do" list—like a
shopping list—which should have helped you plan how to spend your
time to the best effect.

Rule 2: Do Not Attempt too Much

Most people find that they can only organize up to about half their
time, as other people and unexpected events take up much of your time.
Just make sure these do not become an excuse for not getting things done!

Rule 3: Start Now

Do not procrastinate!

Rule 4: Reward Yourself

Finally, when you *have* completed something important, reward
yourself in some way. Life should not be all work!

Module 6: Developing Professional Attributes

Key concept

identifying and understanding those attributes which are the hallmarks of being a professional in your area

Learning outcomes

On completing this module you will have:

- *identified attributes of professionalism*
- *internalized professional attributes*

Task 1: Identifying Professional Attributes

The concept of professionalism is frequently different from one profession to another. Think about your own profession, then identify some of its values and attributes and its role in society.

_____

_____

_____

_____

Task 2: Practicing as an Informed Professional

What professional attributes and values do you need to demonstrate to show that you are ready to take your place as a new member of the profession?

_____

_____

_____

_____

Task 3: Acting Ethically and with Integrity

What constitutes professional conduct in any area is frequently open to interpretation and sometimes widely debated. Think about some of the current leaders in your profession whom you admire and list the professional attributes that they display.

_____

_____

_____

_____

Task 4: Reflecting on Your Own Professional Attributes

List those areas where you feel your own professional attributes and values need to be developed. Suggest some strategies that will allow this development to take place.

_____

_____

_____

_____

Module 7: Setting the Framework for Your Learning Experiences

Key concept

developing a shared view of the workplace experience

Learning outcome

On completing this module you will have:

- *considered expectations and responsibilities of student and supervisor*
- *negotiated learning opportunities*

Task 1: Negotiating Learning Opportunities

Revisit your stated career goals in relationship to this work experience.

a)   How might this organization contribute to these goals?

_____

_____

_____

_____

b)   Identify your desired learning outcomes for this work experience.

_____

_____

_____

_____

Task 2: Identifying Expectations and Responsibilities

After discussing these outcomes with your supervisor, revise them in terms of what the organization can provide.

_____

_____

_____

_____

Module 8: Evaluating Organizational Culture

Key concept

identifying elements of organizational culture

Learning outcomes

On completing this module you will have:

- *gained an understanding of workplace culture*
- *identified aspects that contribute to or detract from the effective management of organizational culture*
- *identified models of effectively managing organizational culture*

Task 1: Describe Your View of the Workplace's Organizational Culture. Remember That Organizational Culture Includes the Informal as Well as the Formal Processes, So Include in Your Discussion Two Aspects of Each. What Effect Did These Aspects Have on the Organization?

_____

_____

_____

Task 2: What Are the Principles That You Can Identify That Contribute to Effectively Managing Organizational Culture?

_____

_____

_____

Task 3: What Are the Things That Sometimes Work against the Effective Management of Workplace Culture?

_____

_____

_____

Task 4: In an Ideal Environment What Do You Think Are the Key Contributors to Effective Organizational Culture?

_____

_____

_____

Module 9: Communicating with Your Workplace Supervisor

Key concept

maximizing communication opportunities

Learning outcomes

On completing this module you will have considered the importance of:

- *planning opportunities for communication*
- *seizing opportunities for communication*
- *developing effective communication*

Task 1: Why Is It Important That Effective Communication between You and Your Supervisor Is Maintained?

_____

_____

_____

What Would Make This Communication Effective?

_____

_____

Task 2: Identify a Number of Types of Communication in Which You and Your Supervisor Could Engage.

_____

_____

_____

_____

Case Study

Michael had been very excited when he was taken on by the local newspaper for work experience. As a final year journalism student he saw this as getting a "foot in the door" which hopefully might lead to a permanent position after graduation. The editor had assigned him to Peter Jurgens, the sports editor, for the duration of the work experience, and this too was an exceptional piece of good luck. Peter Jurgens had an excellent professional reputation and Michael felt he would learn great a deal from him, particularly as he didn't really know very much about sports journalism and had never seen himself working in this field. Michael hadn't actually been able to speak to Peter before starting at the newspaper because Peter was always too busy to see him, but Michael was sure it would be alright once he started and was given something to do.

Michael began work on a Monday, and as this was a "low sports news day" Peter always took Mondays off. No one else in the office seemed to know that Michael was starting and didn't have anything ready for him to do. An enterprising office assistant took the opportunity of having an extra pair of hands available and asked Michael to complete the photocopying and then start on the enormous backlog of filing. Although this wasn't exactly what Michael had hoped for, he did what he was asked because he felt things would be different when Peter arrived on Tuesday. However, things didn't really change very much. Peter didn't have time to talk to Michael when he arrived at work because he had a deadline to meet. Michael started to feel very conspicuous just standing around the office, but tried to look busy so he wouldn't be asked to do the rest of the filing.

After lunch Peter had a couple of appointments out of the office and said it wouldn't be appropriate for Michael to accompany him. He asked the receptionist to "keep an eye on him," so it was more filing. Wednesday was a little better because Peter asked him to go to the library and research through some back issues of the paper. Feeling that he was at last doing something that resembled real journalism, Michael was pleased with himself when he went to Peter's office to give him what he had found. Peter had someone with him and his secretary told Michael she would give it to Peter when he was free. Then, more filing. At least it was better than sitting around trying to look busy! Peter never mentioned the research to Michael so he never really knew whether it was useful or not.

By now Michael was feeling very frustrated and thought he should say something to Peter but didn't quite know how to approach it. He had never been able to get more than a quick word with Peter as he hurried through the office, let alone the opportunity to discuss the work experience. Michael felt very dejected and began to doubt that he wanted to work in the industry at all.

Task 3: What Steps Could Michael Have Taken Prior to Starting This Work Experience That Might Have Made Things Proceed Differently?

_____

_____

_____

Task 4: What Could Michael Do at This Stage to Open Up the Lines of Communication with Peter?

_____

_____

_____

_____

Module 10: Learning from Your Workplace Supervisor

Key concept

identifying strategies for learning from the workplace supervisor

Learning outcomes

On completing this module you will be able to:

- *identify opportunities for learning*
- *plan learning experiences*
- *reflect on learning experiences*

Task 1: Identifying Opportunities for Learning

Considering your personal goals and the identified skills and attributes you wish to acquire, nominate three types of workplace behavior which you feel would enhance your career.

_____

_____

_____

_____

Task 2: Planning Learning Experiences

With your workplace supervisor, consider how you could develop enhanced workplace behavior. Nominate three activities below, including the timing and implementation of these.

_____

_____

_____

_____

Task 3: Reflecting on Your Experience

Take time to reflect on your three activities. What were the most successful aspects, and if improvements could be made, what would these be?

_____

_____

_____

_____

Module 11: Dealing with Conflict
in the Workplace

> ## Key concept
>
> *understanding the nature of conflict and developing
> strategies for its resolution*
>
> ## Learning outcomes
>
> On completing this module you will be able to:
>
> - *clarify conflict*
> - *identify strategies for managing conflict*
> - *prevent conflict*

The case study, "Dealing with Conflict in the Workplace," is designed
to assist you in clarifying conflict, identifying strategies for managing
conflict, and preventing conflict.   Read through the case study then
reflect on the tasks.

Dealing with Conflict in the Workplace: A Case Study

Jane sighed wearily and shut down her computer for the day. It
was already an hour past five and she'd promised herself to leave on
time today, but here she was *again*.

"Jane!" she heard her name being called. "Could you please come
to my office so that I can explain how I'd like for tomorrow's meeting
to be set up?"

Jane considered ignoring Susan Birch's call. After all, it *was* six
o'clock. "ll be there in a moment," she replied, with just a tinge of
irritation.

Susan appeared at her door before she could make a move. "*Well*,
Jane, I'm not asking much—you know how important this meeting is
tomorrow morning. I'm surprised that you find it so inconvenient to
give me a bit of assistance."

"It's not that I don't want to help, Susan. It's just that for the last
two weeks I've had to stay after work, and I've also come in early as
well at your request. I can't help feeling that this extra time wouldn't be

necessary if you'd simply let me know in advance what's required so that I could plan accordingly. As far as the meeting tomorrow, I have the papers for the meeting all prepared—it will only take a minute to set up the room in the morning."

"So you say, Jane, but you know I always like to review procedures for important meetings. It's worth the time. Your problem is that you don't manage your time during the day. If you did, then the extra time wouldn't be required. For example, I've noticed that you consistently take personal phone calls, you chat off and on all day with others in the office, I can never find you at your desk when I need you, and you put off the tasks that you dislike doing—many of these very important to an efficient office."

"Susan, that's very unfair. If you're unhappy with the way I'm doing my job, you should let me know. *You* should know that the office is buzzing about how you treat us, expecting us to give up lunch hours, come in early, and stay late, day after day. And even then, you're never satisfied with the work we do for you! Several of us have put in an official complaint about what we consider to be unreasonable demands and expectations."

"For your information, Jane, two weeks ago I put several of you on notice to the supervisor. No doubt these would be the same persons who have put in a complaint about me! It will be interesting to see the outcome of all these complaints."

Task 1: Clarifying the Conflict

What do you believe are the underlying issues and problems surrounding the conflict described in the scenario?

_____

_____

_____

_____

Task 2: Considering Problem-Solving Strategies

Considering the scenario, apply the following strategies for managing conflict:

a) Describe the views and feelings of both Jane and Susan.

_____

_____

_____

_____

b) Considering their views and feelings, as well as the issues and problems, briefly state five alternative ways to resolve this conflict.

_____

_____

_____

_____

Task 3: Preventing Conflict

What workplace strategies could assist in preventing conflicts such as these from arising?

_____

_____

_____

_____

Module 12: Using Problem-Based Learning

Key concept

developing problem-solving strategies for the workplace

Learning outcomes

On completing this module you will have:

- *researched and analyzed problems in professional practice*
- *developed effective solutions to problems*
- *managed group processes for effective results*

Problem-based learning (PBL) is a student-centered learning strategy which is ideally suited to both individual and group experiential learning. It places problems, queries, or puzzles particular to the profession at the center of learning. With PBL as the focus, case studies can be used for students to analyze, research, and present for discussion. Using this learning strategy, the educator in charge of the experiential learning experience can locate or create one or a series of case studies to explore issues in the workplace. Below are sample materials using PBL and case studies as learning strategies. The subject being studied in this instance is Management of Archives. WebCT, a computer mediated communication tool, facilitates the teaching and learning. The sample material is included below.

For students, the material

- includes a rationale for PBL
- describes how to manage and approach the case study
- advises on monitoring and fulfilling assessment guidelines
- details how to present and participate in the case study analysis
- details the learning outcomes
- outlines the criteria by which the case study is assessed
- provides an example of a case study written for the course
- provides an evaluation form to evaluate group work processes

For educators, the material includes the Educator's Assessment Form.

Case Study Guide for the Student

Why Are We Using Case Studies?

Management of Archives will be using case studies to explore the content, problems, issues, and challenges in this field. The subject has been designed around the principles of problem-based learning (PBL) using case studies involving group work as the primary learning strategy. PBL is centered around meaningful, "real-life" experiences. PBL encourages you to apply the knowledge and experience you presently have, to determine what knowledge you don't have but need to address problems, and to apply these towards resolving problems presented. PBL encourages you to develop critical thinking and problem-solving skills that you can apply throughout your life. Its main goal is to enhance your professional performance by building your confidence, skills, and knowledge in a particular discipline.

What Are the Special Features of PBL?

PBL builds strong links between your university studies and the workplace by:

- linking knowledge and learning to relevant, real-world contexts
- studying major concepts in an engaging way
- encouraging you to apply critical thinking and problem-solving skills
- enhancing your research capabilities in analyzing workplace problems
- enhancing your ability to work for group outcomes
- enhancing your communication skills
- encouraging you to perform as a professional

How Can You Best Manage Your Case Study?

The workplace expects people to be able to work effectively as group members, so it's worth developing effective strategies to do that while at university. This section describes how you might manage the group experience in this subject.

A case study requires you to work as a group. You can individually research problems and issues in the case study, but these then need to be considered in relation to each other. This means group interaction.

To make contact easier for you, a WebCT discussion board site will be set up for you and locked so that only members of your group can access it. There you can share ideas and attach drafts of material, Powerpoint slides, or other material in preparation for your case study presentation.

Remember there may be several "solutions" and effective strategies appropriate for your case study. A group process can canvass various options in a way individuals cannot. Your goal is to present a well researched, thoughtfully considered, carefully argued, reasonable, and possibly innovative and original solution.

Remember: a case study resolution is only as good as your group effort.

As a group, you will need to

- decide how you will communicate
- record actions at face-to-face or virtual meetings
- determine how the workload will be shared
- decide who will do what
- take individual interests and strengths into consideration, where possible
- keep sufficient records to submit for your Individual Contribution Statements and your group assessment of individual contribution

Possibly, you may have not worked in this way before, so your tutors are keen to support your efforts. There will be time during the tutorials in weeks 2 through 12, after formal presentations, to have group sessions with your tutor, or you may use this time to meet with members of your group. It is anticipated that there will be approximately 20-30 minutes remaining in the tutorials for this type of interaction. You may also contact your tutor at other times should this not be enough time.

Checklist for Approaching Your Case Study

This checklist will help you monitor your group progress and fulfill the assessment requirements.

First, as individuals:

❏   carefully read and reflect on the case study

Then, as a group:

❏   identify the nature of the problem using brainstorming, concept mapping, or other group processes to bring out individual views

❏   ask questions about what you don't understand

❏   state what you individually know is relevant to the case study

❏   identify the concepts, issues, and problems using your group knowledge from previous experiences and subjects studied

❏   state what you don't know collectively

❏   identify the resources you need to research the case study

❏   design an action plan to reveal relevant aspects of the case study

❏   agree on research tasks required

❏   agree on individual and group responsibilities

❏   agree on progress checkpoints, deadlines, and meetings (face-to-face and virtual)

❏   develop a work plan for completing the case study requirements

As you continue work on your case study:

❏   share your research at various checkpoints

❏   bring together all relevant research and reconsider your case study

❏   identify any remaining gaps in your research

❏   bring together all your completed material

❏   incorporate your research into your analysis of the case study

Preparing for your case study tutorial presentation:

❏   gain feedback on your ideas with your tutor at tutorials

❏   consider how your case study should be presented at the tutorial

❏   agree on two focus questions to post for WebCT discussion

❏   appoint moderators in your group to respond to WebCT discussion

- ❑ compile your bibliography and complete your annotations
- ❑ rehearse your presentation
- ❑ present your case study analysis to your tutorial group

Your Group Work Evaluation Form is included in your Self-Study resources in WebCT.

Presentation and Submission Requirements for Your Case Study

For the WebCT component:

1. choose two focus questions to highlight major aspects of your case study
2. decide on your 10 "best" readings (citations only) for your case study
3. post your questions and best readings (1 and 2 above) on the WebCT discussion board by noon on Monday, 7 days before your case study presentation
4. appoint one or more group members to moderate and provide critical response to the WebCT comments during the 7 days
5. close discussion the following Monday at noon
6. note major points made during the WebCT discussion for inclusion in your case study presentation

For Your Case Study Presentation at the Tutorial

7. Present your case study.

   Present on your appointed Tuesday using 25 minutes for your presentation and 15 minutes for interactive discussion with members of the tutorial. Note that you should prepare to facilitate discussion in some provocative way that ensures interaction. You could, for example, include interaction throughout your 40 minute time period.

8. Submit an annotated bibliography.

   Include at least 20 sources with annotations between 40-50 words for each item.

9. Submit your group assessment.

Submit to the tutor, at the tutorial one week after the presentation, a one-page statement with an agreed upon mark out of 10 percent for each individual, along with bullet points highlighting each individual's contribution from the group's perspective. Group members' Individual Statements of Contribution should also be submitted to the tutor.

Participation in Case Studies Other Than Your Own

You are required to:

1. post on the WebCT discussion board a reading/commentary on each of the four case studies other than your own. Ideally you should cite sources to support your views.

2. print out and submit to your tutor your two *best* WebCT discussion board readings/comment any time before week 14 for assessment

3. participate in discussion of the case study when presented at the tutorial

Learning Outcomes and Criteria Used to Assess Your Case Study

1. annotated background readings that indicate the item's usefulness to the case study

2. effective integration of your research into your analysis of the case study

3. clear expression of the problems and issues

4. understanding of the concepts included in the case study

5. well-argued rationale for your proposed solution

6. response to WebCT discussion revealing a synthesis and critical analysis of others' commentary on your case study

7. evidence of problem-solving skills

8. evidence of critical thinking

9. effective communication skills

10. evidence of effective group work and division of workload

Sample Case Study: Women's Work Museum

The following analysis points should be used to initially focus your research for this case study. Other aspects may emerge as your research continues.

Analysis Points

1. developing acquisition policies
2. applying principles of arrangement and description for private papers
3. considering institutional obligations towards donors
4. considering institutional obligations towards researchers
5. ensuring the integrity of materials
6. analyzing archivists' ethical responsibilities

The Wylong District included farming, diary, and wine production. Typically, there were many families who had come to the region from overseas, settled there, and never left. Over the years, there were many district annual events and traditional get-togethers that further cemented family relationships. It was common for four generations to have lived in the same area, and even in the same house. Back in 1960, during their annual Spring Festival, the women in the community were sharing stories about life in the days of their parents, grandparents, and great-grandparents. They reminisced for hours about their families making jams, jellies, pickles, and relish; making handicrafts—clothing, bedding, knitting, and quilting; and the amazing number of kitchen utensils and cooking pots, and all the cleaning. And so many of them kept daily diaries. Who would have time to do that these days? What they realized was the amazing amount of family records and artifacts they all had stored away in their homes. There were similarities, but just as many items reflected the culture of their families' home country. Those kids today—they don't know what hard work is—they should have lived back then! The women realized they had a fascinating social history which should be preserved. They felt sure that school children, as well as many others, would enjoy seeing and perhaps experiencing "women's work" in some way. That's it! Let's call it the Women's Work Museum!

The Wylong District Council was approached for a location and some funding to develop the collection. This is all history now. A Women's Work Museum Committee formed in those early days. They established written guidelines for collection development and strategies for appraising items to be accepted into the collection. Committee members visited several museums and noted successful practices which they implemented. Two attended short courses on arranging and describing museum items. Since 1970, the Women's Work Museum has had a part-time position for a person with training in archives and museum curatorship.

Recently, the Women's Work Museum was offered a real treasure: the family papers of Hilda and Victor Schultz and their ancestors. The papers covered four generations: box after box after box of papers. The Schultz family had documented their lives through diaries and letters between family members still overseas and those in Australia. They kept birth, death, health, and school reports. There were ledgers of expenses, contracts of employment, insurance papers, maintenance of the house and farm equipment, and, according to family lore, an unpublished family history, written by Grandpa Benno, although no one could ever remember seeing it. Hilda and Victor explained to the archivist that they really weren't too sure what was included in the early family history, but felt sure the collection would be a valuable addition to the Women's Work Museum collection.

The archivist, Rosie Argent, murmured encouragingly, promising to contact the Schultz family after a preliminary appraisal. Rosie found the papers extraordinarily rich and complementary to the Museum's collection, but after a preliminary appraisal, realized there could be problems. She pointed out some privacy issues and asked the family how they would like to handle these. It all seemed so distant and removed from the Schultz life today, that they weren't worried and said access would be no problem. Rosie had a work experience student who was studying archives, and together over the next six months, they created a finding aid for the Schultz Family Papers. As Rosie and the student worked on the papers, they noticed some controversial family stories, even judging by today's standards.

Six months later, two things happened simultaneously. Two family members distantly related to the Schultz family and living interstate descended on the Schultz papers, thrilled to discover some rather shocking family stories, especially well detailed in Grandpa Benno's history, which they found. They hastily photocopied various documents and announced to the archivist their intention to publish a "fascinating family expose" in Australia's genealogical society journal.

Then the Schultz's overseas relations came to visit. They were astonished and very angry to find the family papers in the Women's Work Museum. Why weren't they consulted, they demanded. They insisted that the archivist should give them the Schultz Family Papers from the years 1910-1920. They would probably return them, they said, but they just needed to check a few details and possibly remove or add explanatory notes.

Educator's Assessment Form

Management of Archives Case Study

Students: _____

Tutor's Comments on Learning Outcomes and Assessment Criteria	Mark
1. Annotated background readings that indicate the item's usefulness to the case study	
2. Effective integration of your research into your analysis of the case study	
3. Clear expression of the problems and issues	
4. Understanding of the concepts included in the case study	
5. Well-argued rationale for your proposed solution	

Tutor's Comments on Learning Outcomes and Assessment Criteria	Mark
6. Response to WebCT discussion revealing a synthesis and critical analysis of others' commentary on your case study	
7. Evidence of problem-solving skills	
8. Evidence of critical thinking	
9. Effective communication skills	
10. Evidence of effective group work and division of workload	

Tutor: Overall Mark:

Group Work Evaluation Form for Students

As a group, discuss this evaluation of group work as a guide to achieving a good group process. Then, after you have completed your case study, work through this evaluation individually and share your results with the group. See if you can reach a consensus on the score for each item.

		Disagree Strongly			Agree Strongly	
1)	Group meetings were held regularly and everyone attended.	1	2	3	4	5
2)	We talked about and shared the same goals for group work.	1	2	3	4	5
3)	We spent most of our meeting time talking business, but discussions were open-ended and active.	1	2	3	4	5
4)	We talked through any conflicts and disagreements until they were resolved.	1	2	3	4	5
5)	Group members listened carefully to one another.	1	2	3	4	5
6)	We really trusted each other, speaking personally about what we really felt.	1	2	3	4	5
7)	Leadership roles were rotated and shared, with people taking initiative at appropriate times for the good of the group.	1	2	3	4	5
8)	Each member found a way to contribute to the final work product.	1	2	3	4	5
9)	I was really satisfied being a member of the group.	1	2	3	4	5
10)	We freely gave each other credit for jobs well done.	1	2	3	4	5
11)	Group members gave and received feedback to help the group do even better.	1	2	3	4	5

12) We held each other accountable;
    each member was accountable to
    the group.   1   2   3   4   5

13) Group members respected each
    individual's unique contribution
    and talents.   1   2   3   4   5

_____ Total Score _____

Interpreting Your Score

If you scored 52 or greater, your group experiences authentic teamwork, congratulations! If you scored between 39 and 51, there was a positive group identity that might have been developed even further. If you scored between 26 and 38, group identity was weak and probably not very satisfying. If you scored below 26, it was hardly a group at all, resembling a loose collection of individuals. Remember, teamwork doesn't happen by itself. It is a collective responsibility to make the group work effectively.

Module 13: Accepting and Reflecting on Constructive Feedback

Key concept

valuing feedback as a tool in the learning process

Learning outcomes

On completing this module you will understand the importance of:

- *accepting and managing constructive feedback*

Task 1: Remember a Time When You Reacted Negatively to Feedback. Play the Role of an Observer to the Session and Identify the Problems Associated with It.

_____

_____

_____

What Could Each Person Have Done to Make the Session More Effective?

The person giving the feedback could:

_____

_____

_____

The person receiving the feedback could:

_____

_____

_____

Task 2: Reconstruct the Feedback Session So That It Becomes a Positive Experience.

_____

_____

_____

_____

Task 3: What Can You Identify as the Principles of Effective Feedback?

_____

_____

_____

_____

_____

Module 14: Reflecting on Your Work Experience or Internship

Key concept

evaluating your work experience or internship

Learning outcomes

On completing this module you will be able to:

- *identify areas of learning and personal growth*
- *evaluate the degree of learning and personal growth*
- *evaluate the reasons for learning goals not met*

Task: Rating Your Work Experience

Take five minutes to think back over your work experience or internship. Identify aspects of learning and/or personal growth and development that have taken place under the general headings of:

knowledge

_____

_____

skills

_____

_____

attitudes

_____

_____

On a scale of 1 to 10, with 10 being the highest, rate the value of your work experience or internship as a learning experience and note the factors that influenced your decision.

Rating: _____

Factors: _____

_____

_____

_____

In the terms of your stated learning goals, indicate the extent to which each learning goal was achieved.

	Beyond Expectations	Met Expectations	Expectations Not Met
Goal 1			
Goal 2			
Goal 3			
Goal 4			

If any learning goals were not met, what factors contributed to this and what could you possibly have done differently?

_____

_____

_____

_____

Module 15: Matching the Job
with Your Skills

Key concept

locating information about jobs and understanding advertisements

Learning outcomes

On completing this module you will be able to:

- *identify information sources about jobs*
- *match your skills to job advertisements*

Task 1: Finding Information about Jobs

Assume that you are seeking a job as an entry level professional in your field then collect four advertisements, notices or descriptions from the following types of sources:

- Printed material including newspapers and trade journals, Yellow Pages, directories, career libraries
- Internet sources
- Employment agencies
- Professional associations' publications
- Community and local organizations
- Direct sources including your previous work experience, prospective employers, and possible job leads from people you know

Task 2: Matching Your Skills to the Job

Take two of these job "advertisements" and using your own list of skills, briefly state on the following page what skills, knowledge, and attributes you would contribute to this position.

Position 1

_____

_____

_____

_____

_____

Position 2

_____

_____

_____

_____

_____

Module 16: Creating Resumes

Key concept

understanding the resume as a marketing and communication tool

Learning outcomes

On completing this module you will be able to:

* *write a resume which communicates*

Your resume "markets" your knowledge, skills, and experience in a clear, precise, and informative way. It represents what you have accomplished, what you can contribute, and where you are headed. There are standard headings included in resumes, with variations depending on your achievements so far, the type of position for which you may be applying, and your own assessment of the most relevant information and appropriate format for the resume.

Task 1: Analyzing Effective Resumes

a) Locate published materials with examples of resumes. List below the headings and details which you believe would be most effective and relevant for a general resume which highlights your particular strengths.

---

b) Notice the layout and presentation of the resume examples. What features did you find attractive that you would include in your resume?

Task 2: Creating a Draft Resume and Seeking Feedback

Using the Guidelines for Creating Resumes, select appropriate headings based on your analysis of the published materials in task 1 and your own preferences, then create a draft resume. Share your draft with a friend or submit your draft to a careers/employment group which offers advice. Ask for sections which could be enhanced and specific suggestions for improvement. Note the suggestions for enhancement.

_____

_____

_____

Task 3: Improving Your Resume

Considering the areas suggested for enhancement and after seeking guidance from published materials to assist you, redraft your resume. Ask for a second round of feedback.

_____

_____

_____

Module 17: Applying for Your First Position

Key concept

writing the best possible job application

Learning outcomes

On completing this module you will be able to:

* *address the selection criteria*

Each time you apply for a job, you must tailor your application to meet the criteria for the job. The responsibility is yours to demonstrate that your particular experience, skills, and qualifications equip you to meet those required by the job.

Most job advertisements, especially government departments, statutory bodies, and universities, list the main FUNCTIONS of the job (or provide an outline of its key DUTIES) and provide a statement of the ESSENTIAL and DESIRABLE CRITERIA for the position. A detailed package including the above information is usually available from the contact person, and you can arrange to obtain this job application package when you make your initial enquiries about the position.

Your aim in writing the job application is to demonstrate how your experience, skills, and qualifications meet the criteria. If you have prepared well, you will have analyzed your own skills and abilities and will be aware of your own strengths and weaknesses. You will also have analyzed the requirements of the job and have decided that you are capable of meeting those requirements. Your task now is to put that capacity on paper as clearly and concisely as possible to convince the selection panel that you are worthy of further consideration.

Addressing a lengthy list of selection criteria is a daunting prospect for most job seekers.

To succeed requires:
- careful assessment of the job
- good understanding of your academic and personal strengths
- quality written communication skills
- considerable time, energy, and effort

The reward may be a well-paid and satisfying graduate career.

Some Responses to Typical Selection Criteria

a)   Demonstrated skills in oral and written communication

    i)   Unsatisfactory response

        I have well-developed oral and written communication skills. All of the positions I have occupied in my ten years in the department have required that I communicate well in all circumstances.

    ii)   Acceptable response

        Throughout my career in the department I have been involved in work that has required that I communicate effectively with both staff and the public, at all levels. I have prepared written correspondence of all types—letters, ministerials, detailed reports and submissions—and would be happy to provide examples for the panel's perusal, if required.

        I have also been required to communicate orally with a range of individuals and groups, ranging from members of the public at the registry counter, through employer representatives in the Business Liaison Section, to branch heads and other senior managers in the Personal Services Branch. Matters I have dealt with include: personal enquiries, telephone enquiries, requests for information, counseling of staff, and complaints.

b)   A relevant tertiary qualification

Some criterion only require a brief statement. For example:

In 1994 I successfully completed my bachelor of science degree at Endeavor University. I majored in Marine Biology and secured a grade point average of 4.0 (see academic record attached).

c)   Demonstration of high-level research skills

Some criteria require a more detailed examination of your study, work, and extracurricular activities to show how you meet the criterion. For example, analytical research skills are necessary to complete a law degree, so you could write:

During my studies I undertook over thirty research assignments covering a range of issues. This has developed my ability to recognize and assess legal issues and to complete detailed and relevant research. The quality of my research is demonstrated by my seventy percent average mark for research papers.

d)   High-level interpersonal and communication skills including the ability to consult with other professionals and advise members of the public

Some criteria have more than one element. It is best to address each element individually. For example:

High-level interpersonal skills are necessary to both my voluntary work and my paid work. I have gained experience working and communicating with a wide range of people including scientists, administrators, and members of the public. Specifically, I have undertaken both consultative and advisory roles.

Consultative

During two months work experience with the Department of Environment and Heritage, I was a member of the Turtle 2000 Team, researching turtle hatcheries. This involved consulting with biologists from the Institute of Marine Science, with senior administrators of the Reef Marine Park Authority (RMPA), and with park rangers. I organized three planning meetings and was responsible for briefing participants and collecting and collating their contributions. This process involved numerous phone calls, meetings, and written briefs.

Advisory

My part-time work as a reef guide with Reef Adventures involves advising small groups of tourists on a range of practical and ecological matters. During the boat journey to Deep Reef, I deliver a short talk on the boat's safety features, and then make a slide presentation explaining basic coral reef ecology. Once at Deep Reef I brief tourists about reef dangers, then guide snorkellers through the shallows. This tour includes a commentary explaining all kinds of marine life encountered during the swim. Because of this experience I was also asked by my employer to draft a submission to the Reef Marine Park authority, expressing my view on the future zoning proposals for Deep Reef.

Task: After Obtaining the Information from the Organization, Address the Selection Criteria, Working through the Following Process:

- analyze your own skills and abilities
- read all the supporting material and instructions carefully. The application package usually contains a detailed statement of exactly what the employer is seeking so do not waste the opportunity by not giving the employer what he or she is wanting
- highlight the key words in the criteria. Criteria will often begin with phases like "demonstrated ability to," "proven ability in," "sound knowledge of," or "experience with." Each of these phrases means something different. For example, if the essential criterion requires that you be able to demonstrate that you possess "initiative," you should think about whether you have the ability to identify purposeful work opportunities and take action. Initiative means being a self-starter. To "demonstrate" that you possess this ability, you should refer to situations in your past where you recognized emerging problems, dealt with them, identified the implications of actions, and handled them in an enterprising manner
- broadly assess each criterion. Think of everything you have done that shows how you meet the criterion. You should consider such things as your university studies, paid work, voluntary work, sports, interests, and activities
- address the criteria on an attachment which includes your name and contact details, the position title, and a heading such as "Statement Addressing Selection Criteria"
- with each criterion as a separate heading, explain underneath how you satisfy it. You make the selection panel's task easier if your heading is a complete restatement of each criterion in full. This saves panel members the task of referring to the duty statement as they review your application
- you should explain, clearly and concisely, demonstrating through examples, how your study, work experience, or other activities have given you the knowledge, skills, or experience that meets the criterion

- be concise and specific indicating when, where, and in what situations you have worked
- follow instructions carefully, sending only what has been requested and providing photocopies, not original documents, where required

Presentation

- make sure that the application is neat and easy to read (preferably word processed)
- use topic headings to separate each of the qualifications and your discussion of them
- make good use of "white" space
- be concise—be sure that you provide sufficient evidence to support your claims but do not "waffle"

Length

The length of your application will depend very much on the nature of the job and the number of essential and desirable criteria associated with it.

But remember, the longer the application, the more demanding it becomes for the panel to read through it. Your aim should be to provide sufficient evidence of your ability to meet each qualification without overdoing it.

If There Are No Selection Criteria

If there are no set criteria, you need to research the position and anticipate what the required skills for the position might be. This is then formatted in the same way as your claims to the selection criteria. You may include this information or "skills page" in the body of the resume or as an additional attachment. This skills page will include technical, professional, and personal sills. The majority of skills listed will be your transferable "personal" skills.

Module 18: Understanding the Basics of Cover Letters

Key concept

understanding the key features of cover letters

Learning outcomes

On completing the module you will be able to:
- *identify the key elements of cover letters*
- *create appropriately styled cover letters*

Task 1: Understanding Cover Letters

Cover letters should provide particular information. Selecting either the organization where you are seeking work experience or an advertised position of employment, make notes for a cover letter which will answer the following:

Who you are:

Why you are writing:

Why you are suitable and what contribution you would bring to the organization:

Why you would like to work for this organization:

What material is included with this cover letter:

_____

_____

A concluding "action statement" which indicates what should happen next:

_____

_____

Task 2: Creating the Cover Letter

You should check the following guides to assist you in creating a cover letter.

*   sample cover letters
*   layout for cover letters
*   guidelines for cover letters

After studying these, take one of the job advertisements collected for your "Locating Information about Jobs" module and use it to create a cover letter. You should now proceed to the "Creating Cover Letters" module.

Module 19: Creating Cover Letters

Key concept

marketing yourself through a letter of introduction

Learning outcomes

On completing this module you will be able to:
- *analyze the requirements of effective letters of introduction*
- *select an appropriate style for your letter*

With every application for work experience or employment, you should include a cover letter which introduces yourself. Your letter should
- outline your particular skills and knowledge thus distinguishing you from others
- highlight the special contribution you will make through your personal qualities, experience, and other factors
- indicate high-quality communication and interpersonal skills
- show you have some knowledge of the organization
- reflect your individuality

Task: Creating Letters of Introduction

Type 1: "Cold Canvassing" or "Prospective" and "Referral" Letters

If you are writing a "cold canvassing" letter, you are writing to someone in an organization who is not presently taking on work experience students or actively recruiting to fill a position. The aim here is to market yourself. First, you must research the content for this type of letter by
- identifying likely organizations
- researching the organization's endeavors (see your module "Finding Out about the Workplace," tasks 1 and 2)
- narrowing the field to the best match between yourself and your organization

- identifying the most appropriate person in the organization to receive your letter

Referring to the organization you have nominated as appropriate for your work experience or employment, create a cold canvassing letter of introduction. A slight variation on this form of letter is a referral letter in which someone in an organization has suggested you make an approach. Using the same cold canvassing letter, add an introductory statement in your opening paragraph which identifies the person who referred you to their organization and why the referral is appropriate.

Type 2: "Invited" or "Solicited" Cover Letter

Create an invited or solicited cover letter based on an advertised position. Here you are responding to an advertised position. We know that 20 percent of jobs are advertised. You will be responding to the organization's specific selection criteria as part of your application, but your cover letter should demonstrate a knowledge of the organization through research you have undertaken as well as cover the special qualities you bring to the position and organization. Review your "Making the Most of Your Job Interview" module and the "Guidelines for Cover Letters."

Module 20: Making the Most of Your Job Interview

Key Concept

achieving a successful interview

Learning Outcomes

On completing this module you will be able to:
- *find out about the organization/position*
- *develop an interview strategy*
- *achieve a strong interview performance*

If you are called for an interview, congratulate yourself: you have met the essential criteria! Now on to the interview. The prime purpose of a job interview is to evaluate your suitability for a particular job. Information may be shared, goals and responsibilities clarified, but essentially you are being evaluated. So how can you prepare to demonstrate you are the best person for the job?

There are three major tasks in achieving a successful interview: researching the organization/position; projecting yourself; and preparing for the interview itself. This module provides an opportunity for you to practice and hone your skills.

Task 1: Researching the Organization/Position

To demonstrate that you are the most appropriate person for the job, you need to know how you match up with the organization. Find an advertised position in your field in a newspaper, and then find information about the organization offering the job. Research the following:
- goals, vision, mission, strategic plan, business plan
- history and future
- organizational structure
- size, sections, associated organizations

Check these out as possible sources of information on the organization:
- annual reports
- histories

- web pages
- brochures
- organization's applications
- newsletters
- reputation as judged by experts—newspaper and journal articles

Task 2: Developing an Interview Strategy

You have already submitted a cover letter and a statement addressing the selection criteria for the position. Review these, then consider the following:

a) What are the three most important points you want to get across in the interview?

_____

_____

_____

_____

b) What are your strengths you want to emphasize for this position?

_____

_____

_____

_____

c) What you want to minimize?

_____

_____

_____

_____

Task 3: Considering Typical Interview Questions

a) Consult the Typical Interview Questions sheet. Pick one easy
    question and jot down a brief answer.

_____

_____

_____

_____

_____

b) Nominate a question you would find particularly difficult to answer.

_____

_____

_____

c) Make an attempt to answer it.

_____

_____

_____

_____

Task 4: Rehearsing the Interview

Ask two or three friends to create a mock interview panel. Using the
advertised position, cover letter, and application you have written, try to
answer some of the questions from the Typical Interview Questions. Ask
your friends to create two questions specific to the position. Afterwards,
evaluate your performance together.

What areas could have been improved?

_____

_____

_____

_____

What would you do differently?

_____

_____

_____

_____

Task 5: Exploring Job Requirements

Usually you will be asked if you have any questions about the position. You might ask for more details about the job or whether there are staff development programs.

Nominate two further questions which you could ask.

_____

_____

_____

_____

Resume Presentation: Layout

There is no set format, but the aim is to achieve a resume that is easy to read, logically organized, attractive, and consistent in look. Ensure you use wide margins and generous spacing. Add your name along with a page reference as a heading for each page.

Resume Presentation: Headings

There are standard headings used in most resumes. Select those which would highlight your particular strengths or explain why you are particularly suitable for a position. Those listed in chapter 10 are the most common ones used along with the information below that should be included.

Personal Details

Your name

Address

Telephone number

Facsimile and e-mail address (if available)

Citizenship or residential status

Optional items include date of birth, gender, marital status, ethnic background, religion

10

Creating Resumes

Education/Qualifications/Honors/Prizes

- Name and location of educational institution
- Date and name of degree earned, including specialization, if appropriate
- Professional courses if qualifications earned (details as above)
- Scholarships/honors/prizes/awards including title, date earned, and a brief explanatory note
- Optional items include a list of units studied and marks achieved; alternatively include an academic transcript as an attachment

Professional Work Experience

Placing the emphasis on experience most relevant to the position, provide for each work experience undertaken the following details:

- name and location of employer
- period of work experience
- brief listing of major duties performed and skills acquired/practiced
- major achievements

Voluntary Work Experience

For each separate description of voluntary work experience include the items listed above in Professional Work Experience. Your voluntary work experience could include experience within clubs, professional associations, community organizations, and other such groups.

Prospective employers are also looking for generic skills applicable across various jobs, so include examples within your professional and voluntary work experience which highlight the following about yourself:

- well developed written and oral communication skills
- organizational skills
- interpersonal skills of high order
- ability to work as a team member
- commitment
- leadership
- initiative

Competencies, Technical and Professional Skills

If you are applying for your first professional position after graduation, you may wish to indicate generic skills you have gained as a result of your degree course. Check the Analyzing Your Skills module for guidance.

Here list specific skills such as your computing competency, language proficiency, proficiency with database management, or research capabilities.

Depending on your own background and the type of position for which you are applying, other items to include could be membership in professional organizations, administrative skills exhibited, positions held, publications, consultancies, research, and projects.

Memberships in Professional Associations and Organizations

List professional organizations, associations, clubs, societies and other groups to which you belong, including any offices held or official positions. Generally, feature prominently those relevant to the position for which you are applying.

Other Activities

Some resumes include your interests and hobbies such as traveling, karate, photography, etc., but carefully consider whether these add strength to the other information you are providing.

References/Referees

It is customary to include the names, organizations, addresses, and contact details for two or three persons who can each comment on different aspects about you such as your personal, technical, and professional skills. Be sure to ask their permission before including them on your resume, and it is usual practice to inform them about the position and to supply them with a copy of your application, if requested.

Statement about Your Career/Professional Goals

Including such a brief statement often focuses attention on your long-term objectives and may assist the organization is matching their goals with yours. You may include such information in your cover letter or close to the beginning of your resume.

Completing Application Forms

Some employers provide application forms for all candidates to complete. This may be to provide some standardization that will streamline the handling of applications or facilitate the ranking of applicants. But it probably is also a test of

- how concisely and clearly you write
- how well you can answer questions set by the employer
- how well you have developed specific skills and qualities which are important to that employer

It is important then that you give due care in completing the application form. Some guiding principles include:

- photocopy the form and prepare a draft before completing the official form
- read through the entire application form before you start writing
- identify areas where you can highlight your strengths as well as those questions which are potential weaknesses
- use examples from your past to highlight the skills for which the employer is looking
- provide exactly the information requested

- ensure that your response is relevant where you are asked a particular question
- mark any sections that are not relevant "n/a"
- use black ink as it photocopies more clearly
- write or type? Unless the form actually specifies, it doesn't matter. You may wish to type your responses on a separate sheet of paper that is the same size as the space provided and paste that on the form. For other employers, you can attach a separate sheet and continue your answer on that. You may prefer to print your replies
- attach a copy of your resume, particularly if the application form has not given you sufficient scope to talk about your suitability for the position
- attach a cover letter

Guidelines for Cover Letters

Use these guidelines to create your cover letters. You may be applying for work experience or an advertised position, so the guidelines below should be selected based on the type of letter you are writing.

Content
- identify the particular position for which you are applying or the section within which you seek work experience
- identify all key requirements in the job advertisement
- examine your resume and find examples to meet these requirements
- include a few specific examples
- state clearly why your knowledge, skills, and attributes contribute to the organization
- use concrete examples rather than generalities
- display an air of confidence
- quantify and illustrate your strengths
- highlight your resume but avoid repetition
- emphasize only qualities relevant to the position
- reveal your individuality

- conclude purposefully, asking for particular action such as an interview

Language

- capture the reader's interest with your opening statement
- use concise and clear language, avoiding words which could be interpreted incorrectly
- use "plain English"
- use a "conservative" style, with no contractions, incomplete sentences, or slang
- avoid clichés and hackneyed phrases
- use strong verbs which demonstrate action and accomplishments
- create a natural, logical flow of information
- aim for a lively, energetic style
- show positive and avoid negative attitudes
- avoid limiting your accomplishments
- edit carefully, eliminating all unnecessary words
- ensure spelling and grammar are correct
- seek comments on your language from others before finalizing
- read your materials from a perspective employer's viewpoint—is your message compelling?

Length

- aim for brevity and conciseness
- keep your opening paragraph short, no longer than eight lines
- use a single standard-sized page preferably
- add additional pages addressing selection criteria if required for the job.

Presentation

- word process or type your material
- use standard-sized bond paper in white, cream, or other "conservative" look
- use an envelope that allows your application to be unfolded

Layout for Cover Letters

Date
Leave 4 lines

Home Address
Street
City, State, and Zip Code
Tel: (Home and Work)
E-mail:
Leave 2 lines

Name
Job Title
Company Name
Postal Address including
City, State, and Zip Code
Leave 2 lines

Dear (Title and Surname),
Leave 2 lines

Body of Letter (See Stylistic Guidelines for Cover Letters)
Leave 2 lines

Yours sincerely,
Leave 4 lines for your signature

Your name

The usual formal layout for business letters includes:
- justified left margin
- block format with no indents, commas, or periods in the address
- normal business conventions for opening and closing letters

Cover Letter Seeking Work Experience

Date

13 Williams Street
City, State, Zip Code

Tel:

Ms Susan Whatley
Director, Public Relations
Expert Managers Pty Ltd
76 Whiting Street
City, State, Zip Code

Dear Ms Whatley,

I am writing to inquire whether you would be interested in offering work experience for an enthusiastic and committed student. I am currently enrolled in the second year of my Bachelor of Communication degree specializing in Public Relations, and we are required to undertake six weeks work experience. My respect for the Floriade events and the Red Nose Campaign led me to seek work experience with you.

You might ask what I can offer your organization. Throughout my high school and tertiary studies, I have undertaken a variety of paid part-time and voluntary work including salesperson with David Jones, receptionist with Office Systems, research assistant for Canberra and District Historical Society, and telephone survey researcher with Publics Inc. From these I have developed high-level communication skills and have demonstrated my ability to work with a range of people. I would be very interested in contributing these skills and my knowledge of public relations based on my two years of study to your organization.

If you are interested in providing work experience on a voluntary basis for me, your commitment would include assisting me in creating learning experiences, supervising a project which I would undertake to benefit your organization, and providing feedback on my achievements. For your information, I have enclosed a copy of my resume and the unit requirements provided by the lecturer-in-charge. At the end of next week, I will telephone you and discuss with you the possibility of my working for your organization.

Yours sincerely,

Rebecca Smithson

Cover Letter for an Advertised Position

Date

21 Davenport Road
City, State, Zip Code

Ms S Nolan
Graduate Program Coordinator
Ford Motor Company
City, State, Zip Code

Dear Ms Nolan,

Re: Graduate Engineer (Ref: 10/32)

As I am seeking employment with your company (commencing early in 1998). I wish to be considered for placement in the fields of product engineering, manufacturing, and assembly.

Currently, I am in my fourth and final year of study for the degree, Bachelor of Engineering, majoring in Mechanical Engineering.

I have spent nine and a half weeks in vacation employment at the Kalgoorlie Nickel Smelter and relished the challenges inherent to large scale, "real" engineering operations located in more remote regions of the country.

My involvement in the Co-operative Education for Enterprise Development (CEED) scheme, as part of my final Honors project, has led to the gaining of invaluable work experience. In conjunction with the State Energy Commission my task is to 'Design a Demand Actuated District Control Valve' for the metropolitan natural gas network. The project involves the selection and requisition of parts, overseeing the installation and then field-testing in the design, manufacturing, and production aspects of industry, seeing them as a basis for a prosperous and exciting career.

I would welcome the opportunity to work and acquire firsthand experience in my chosen career, under the guidance of a company at the leading edge of technology and dedicated to the advancement of its employees.

Please find enclosed a copy of my curriculum vitae and academic record. I look forward to the opportunity of discussing my application in person.

Yours sincerely,

James Bakerman

Cover Letter for a Nonadvertised Position

Date

7 Banana Court
City, State, Zip Code

Mr Archie Weatherby
Newcastle Investments Unlimited, Inc
City, State, Zip Code

Dear Mr Weatherby,

Please consider this letter as an initial application for a position as an Insurance Broker for Newcastle Investments Unlimited, Incorporated.

I recently graduated from the University of Southern Queensland with a degree in business, where I was president of the Future Business Leaders of Queensland.

Although a recent graduate, I am not a typical new graduate. I attended university in New South Wales and Queensland. I have put myself through these universities by working at such jobs as radio advertising sales and bartending, both of which enhanced my formal education. I have the maturity and ability to embark on a career in insurance brokering, and I would like to do this in New South Wales, the state I grew up in.

I will be in Newcastle at the end of this month and I would like very much to talk with you. I will follow up this letter with a phone call to see if I can arrange a time to meet with you.

Thank you for your consideration.

Yours sincerely,

Jeremy Ogilvy

Job Application Checklist

After addressing the selection criteria and before posting your application, ask yourself the following questions relating to:

1) Your resume

☐ Is your name at the top of each page?

☐ Are your strengths clearly described?

☐ Is your highest educational level shown first in the education section?

☐ Does your skills page provide relevant examples of achievements and activities?

☐ Do your key accomplishments stand out through the use of highlighting?

☐ Have you avoided being too shy or modest in describing yourself and your achievements?

2) Your professional goals (optional)

☐ Does your professional goal statement appear in your resume or is it mentioned in your letter?

☐ Does your professional goal statement clearly and concisely show what sort of work you want?

☐ Is this goal a true indication of your personal ambitions?

☐ Have you described your personal objectives in positive terms?

3) Your cover letter

☐ Is it a personalized original letter rather than a mass-produced copy?

☐ Is it addressed to a named individual? Are the employer's name, title, and address spelled correctly?

☐ Is the letter concise and to the point and no longer than one page?

☐ Have you told the employer what you can do for him rather than what he can do for you?

☐ Have you avoided pleading for favors?

☐ Is your name printed below your signature?

☐ Have you clearly stated the type of employment you are seeking?

☐ Have you avoided an over use of "I"?

☐ Have you indicated that your resume is enclosed?

☐ Have you given some evidence of your research into the prospective employer?

☐ Have you avoided mentioning personal problems?

☐ Have you avoided apologizing for what you do not have?

☐ Does your letter sound insincere or overly flattering?

4) Some general aspects relating to the application

☐ Are your current address and telephone number included?

☐ Have you included an alternative phone number where a message may be left for you?

☐ Have you highlighted specific achievements and experiences (and avoided writing a long autobiography)?

☐ Have you avoided long words, business jargon, terms that you do not normally use?

☐ Have you left out everything negative?

☐ Is every word spelled correctly? Is all grammar, syntax, punctuation, and capitalization correct? Is the letter free of typographical errors?

☐ Does the application address the requirements of the position?

☐ If you're a recent graduate, have you avoided overreliance on your academic achievements?

☐ Have you listed your accomplishments?

☐ Have you used action verbs?

☐ Have you written anything which is difficult to substantiate?

☐ Have you mentioned when you are available for an interview and how you can be contacted?

☐ Have you shown your final draft to two people and sought their opinion?

☐ Is the application neat and attractive?

☐ Is it typed on only one side of each page?

☐ Is the letter and resume on U.S. letterhead?

☐ Is it designed with wide margins and space between para-
   graphs?

☐ Have you found a good quality photocopying machine that
   will make copies on U.S. letterhead?

☐ Is the envelope correctly addressed, with your name and address on the back?

☐ Is the envelope big enough so that you don't have to fold
   your letter?

☐ Have you kept a copy for your job search record?

Typical Interview Questions

Certain questions are frequently asked at interviews. With a particular position in mind, practice answering some of these questions.

1. What attracted you to this position? What would be your contribution?

2. Why do you want to work for this organization?

3. What are your particular strengths?

4. Why do you believe you would be successful in this job?

5. Give examples from your previous experience that have prepared you for this job.

6. Describe two or three achievements and why they gave you satisfaction.

7. What are your major weaknesses, and what have you done to address them?

8. Describe a problem you faced and how you resolved it.

9. Give examples of how you have successfully worked in a team.

10. What led you to this career?

11. What would you see as the ideal job for you?

12. What motivates you?

13. How would you describe yourself?

14. What are your major interests outside work?

15. Where would you see your career in five years time?

Managing a Successful Interview

1   Getting ready

Dress conservatively and groom yourself meticulously.

2   Arriving

Arrive about 15 minutes early, then relax and gather your thoughts.

3   Meeting the panel

The first four minutes appear to be the most important in making an impression. The chair will introduce you to the panel members, and you in turn should shake hands with each person. You will not be expected to remember the panel members' names, but if they have name tags, personalize the interview by addressing them by name.

4   Performing during the interview

Maintain eye contact, smile, remain calm, and demonstrate enthusiasm.

5   Answering the questions

Remain focused on the questions, answer concisely, positively, and confidently using specific examples. Consider pausing to reflect on the question if it is complex, and asking for clarification is acceptable.

6   Turning questions into opportunities

Highlight achievements pertinent to the job. Show your interest in and knowledge of the organization and how you would contribute.

7   Concluding

Take the opportunity to reiterate why you are the person for the job, and conclude by thanking the panel for the interview.

8   Reflecting on your performance

This will not be your only interview! With the experience still fresh in your mind, review how well you did.

- Write down the questions. How well did you answer each one?
- What did you do well in the interview?
- What could you have done better?
- What aspects would you improve and how would you go about doing this?

Student Expression of Interest Form

Name: _____

ID: _____ Phone: _____

Address: _____

_____ Zip code: _____

E-mail: _____

When the time comes to let you know about your placement, we will need to be able to contact you quickly. Please ensure that the contact details you have given are ones that you check on a regular basis. Also, please print your e-mail address very clearly.

1.   What personal strengths are you bringing to the work experience?

_____

_____

2.   What technical strengths are you bringing to the work experience?

_____

_____

3.   What professional strengths are you bringing to the work experience?

_____

_____

4.   What personal strengths would you like to develop during your work experience?

_____

_____

5. What technical strengths would you like to develop during your work experience?

_____

_____

6. What professional strengths would you like to develop during your placement/fieldwork?

_____

_____

7. What other sequence of units have you studied?

_____

_____

8. Please indicate if you have any previous work experience in a relevant area.

_____

_____

Please indicate the type of organization in which you are interested. The placement of students in organizations is dependent on many factors, probably the most important of which is the willingness of the organizations to be involved in the program as well as the student's own strengths and career goals. While every effort will be made to accommodate your wishes it may not be always possible to do so.

9. List up to three types of organizations:

    a. _____

    b. _____

    c. _____

Developing the Plan of Learning Experiences

What is the focus of my work area?

_____

_____

_____

_____

What are the aspects of this work that I would like the student to learn?

1. _____

_____

2. _____

_____

3. _____

_____

4. _____

_____

What are the tasks that I need to provide for the student so he/she can learn the aspects of the work I have identified?

Aspect 1

_____

_____

Aspect 2

_____

_____

Aspect 3

_____

_____

Aspect 4

_____

_____

_____

Commencing and finishing dates

Proposed schedule of consultations between mentor and student for review and evaluation. These are distinct from the more regular workplace and supervision type of instruction and/or feedback situations. While the frequency may vary according to the placement, consultations should occur at strategic times over the year, and the student should be made aware at the beginning of the period when they will occur.

_____

_____

_____

_____

How will the student be supervised? (Sometimes the "formal" mentor is not the day-to-day supervisor. Sometimes the mentoring role is shared.)

_____

_____

_____

_____

11

Example of a
Plan of Learning

This plan provides an excellent example of a mentor who provides both "high challenge" and "high support" as recommended by Daloz (1986). The plan also follows the model's recommendation that structure be provided but that it remain flexible to cater for both the student's individual needs and the opportunities provided by the workplace.

Plan of Learning Example

Student: Sue Patton
Mentor: Ben Jones
Organization: National Sport Information Centre (NSIC)

What Is the Focus of Your Work Area?

The development and maintenance of information systems to help the Australian Sports Commission attain its goals and the NSIC follow its business plan.

What Aspects of This Work Would a Student Need to Explore to Be Able to Understand How It Operates?

1. Understand what types of sport information there are, what types of users there are, and how and why they use information
2. Keeping an eye on what technology is making possible
3. Understanding your organizational setting
4. Balancing the first three points while trying to achieve organizational goals

What Methods Would You Need to Employ and What Tasks Would You Need to Assign to Facilitate This Understanding?

Understand what types of sport information there are, what types of users there are and how and why they use information

- Work in client services area
- Work in information management
- Database maintenance
- Workshopping ideas
- Project planning
- Interface development

Keeping an eye on what technology is making possible

- Self-directed learning
- Location and use of information sources identifying new technologies and innovative applications of existing technologies
- Communication/collaboration with information technology (IT) staff

Understanding your organizational setting

- Awareness of evolving Government Online strategy
- Communication with content creators, information disseminators, management/executive, and internal and external clients
- NSIC's legal imperatives
- NSIC's relationships with other sport information services
- NSIC's obligations as a (mostly) government funded body
- NSIC's obligations as a member of the library community
- NSIC's revenue raising imperatives

Developing workflows, procedures, and systems that can survive without you and that acknowledge that the future will be longer than the present. Thinking in all nine dimensions (i.e., What will go wrong? What can go wrong? Are the payoffs worth the investment? Is there a better way? Should someone else be doing this? Could someone else do it? Does everyone affected know about this? With a little more effort could I kill two birds? Is this bird already dead?).

What Are the Small Tasks That Will Provide the Learning Steps Necessary?

I've identified a number of projects for Sue which incorporate various groupings of the things I think she needs exposure to understand the greater complexity and variety of the work of the IT worker in an information provision setting.

Database Maintenance for Sports Journal Updates

Project Description: This database generates a current awareness service that generates income through subscriptions and document delivery requests. It uses two different subject thesauri in theory but has been corrupted by multiple users adding their own personal touches over the last decade. Sue will be cleaning the database and resolving multiple terminologies by negotiation with indexers. Once clean, this database will be mounted on a web server, and an interface will be designed and developed.

Learning Outcomes

•   Experience in Access 97 (data entry, database design,
    report writing)

•   Use of a subject control tool

•   Negotiation/consultation skills

•   Proofing skills, attention to detail

•   Exposure to design considerations and technical limitations of web
    interfaces to databases

Creating Metadata for ASC Media Releases

Project Description: The Office of Government Online's guidelines for government web sites require metadata for certain types of web documents by 1 December 2000. Sue will be setting up an embedded metadata template in consultation with the information management librarian and the webmaster. She will collecting appropriate documentation, collating subject term lists, and creating in-house procedure documents and providing access to all this via the Australian Sports Commission Intranet.

Learning Outcomes

- Exposure to Dublin Core and AGLS metadata standards
- Web page maintenance
- Metacataloguing experience
- Creation of procedural documentation in a web setting aimed at a professional/technical audience

NSIC Web Archive Project

Project Description: This is an ongoing project which I began in early 1999. Documents are archived on our website and given PURLs. This material is then indexed for inclusion on the AUSPORT database (AUSTROM and Informit Online) and on SPORT Discus with the appropriate PURL so that the indexing database links directly to the full text item. Sue will be involved in identifying suitable items, archiving them, editing them to acknowledge their originators and to be serviceable on our website. There is also scope for indexing the materials.

Learning Outcomes

- Expanded knowledge of information sources in sport
- An exposure to good and bad web techniques when considering portability of web sites
- Negotiation with outside content providers
- Proofing skills, attention to detail in a web setting
- Indexing skills
- Exposure to the workings of hybrid database systems
- Exposure to electronic data interchange in a bibliographic setting
- Hands-on experience with a traditional integrated library management system

Transfer of Serials Binding System to New PC

Project Description: The NSIC's binding contractor provides a proprietary software system for preparing serials binding batches. The PC it is currently stored on is being superseded and the existing data as well as the software need to be transferred to a new PC.

Learning Outcomes

- Experience working with PCs in a networked environment
- Getting used to figuring out software systems you've never seen before
- Troubleshooting without documentation
- Working with a nontechnical user to ascertain technical requirements
- Learning a systematic approach to ad hoc problems
- Exposure to a common area of technical services in a library

These are just starting points. In the information management area a week never goes by without a new opportunity or technology presenting itself. I will be dragging Sue to meetings on and off campus so she can see the variety of demands inherit in this work area. Examples include the AUSTROM Database Provider meetings and the OGO briefings.

She will also be involved in other projects (some of which don't exist yet). For example, I'll be trying to get our picture library on the web and I'm joint leader of an e-commerce pilot project that will be selling AIS goods on our web site. There has also been talk of streaming live video to PCs via a satellite link during the Olympics. New opportunities to learn and practice new skills will arise every week.

Personal Skills

So far this plan of learning has focused on Sue's technical and professional skills and making her aware of the broad and crucial role IT has in the information/knowledge management of any contemporary organization. In terms of personal skills I hope to get Sue to exercise and develop

- Confidence in approaching a problem
- Knowing when you don't know enough and what to do
- Multitasking and getting used to chopping and changing jobs

- Personal organization tools and techniques
- Keeping a sense of humor
- Working with people, speaking their language, translating it for the techos
- Being aware of what's happening with IT and deciding what is important and what isn't and being prepared to constantly review those lists
- Setting priorities (and seeing the grays—like the politics of doing a small unimportant job before a big important job)
- Networking within and outside of an organization

There are other things I would like Sue to reflect on at the end of her placement.

- To know what she does and doesn't like doing
- To know that in a professional position there is room to engineer your job to suit you if you can make those changes benefit your organization
- To have an idea of the sort of job she would like and to have identified the skills she will need to get it and to have acted on a plan to get those skills

Feedback

There will be three formal times when Sue and I will work through the Charting Student Progress Guide together to see how things are going and what things might need attention. Otherwise, we've agreed to touch base briefly each day she's here. If we need a longer time to talk, we'll schedule a special time. Then, of course, there are all those discussions, meetings, and other events where Sue will be coming along with me. So there will be plenty of opportunities for seeing how Sue's doing on an ongoing basis. Ultimately, I'm hoping that Sue will emerge as an independent learner and worker with an ability to recognize what she doesn't know, identify a way to find out what she needs to know, and to know when she's found a good solution.

12

Handbook

Contents

Partners in Learning

Internships for Professional Education In Information Studies

1   What Is PAL?

PAL (Partners in Learning) is an internship program where an undergraduate student in the Information Studies Program at the University of Canberra and an experienced practitioner work together for a specified period of time. Its purpose is to provide the opportunity for the student to become familiar with the professional environment and workplace practices thereby easing the eventual transition from student to practitioner.

It is facilitated by educators and members of the information professions joining together in a collaborative teaching and learning model of education. It is based on the concept that learning is developmental, requires opportunities for practice, critical analysis, reflective thinking, and observing examples of best practice. This model of learning invites students to explore while still providing guidance and encouragement. Facilitated mentoring is an important component of PAL.

As it is essential that all participants in the project share the same goals and expectations, both mentors (workplace supervisors) and academic advisors will undertake training and students will be thoroughly briefed. Mentors and students will be supported throughout the internship by the academic advisors.

2   What Is Mentoring?

Mentoring is not a new concept. Homer recorded what was probably the original mentoring relationship, that between Telemachus and Mentor, the guardian his father Odysseus asked to watch over him when Odysseus left for the siege of Troy. Mentor acted faithfully as teacher, advisor, friend, and surrogate father to Telemachus for the ten years Odysseus was away.

The Greeks believed strongly that we learn skills, culture, and values from other humans whom we look up to or admire. These same principles of mentoring have been important elements in the continuity of art, craft, and commerce from ancient times. The craft guilds of the Middle Ages are a good example. This master/apprentice relationship was eventually transformed into the employer/employee relationship by industrial society.

Today it is possible to identify a number of types of mentoring models, and the one that is intrinsically associated with PAL is that of facilitated mentoring, defined by Murray (1991) as:

> a deliberate pairing of a more skilled or experienced person with a lesser skilled or experienced one, with the agreed-upon goal of having the lesser skilled person grow and develop specific competencies. (xiv)

Murray further states that facilitated mentoring is a structure and series of processes designed to create effective mentoring relationships, guide the desired behavior change of those involved, and evaluate the results for the participants. The PAL project will provide such a structure.

3 Who Benefits?

Mentors benefit through

- participation in students' personal and professional growth thereby receiving intrinsic satisfaction through a sharing of professional skills and knowledge
- enhanced ability to impart skills and knowledge which may further career development
- collaboration in the production of skilled, competent, and leading-edge professionals for the workplace
- opportunities to assess students for future employment
- exposure to current literature and "best practice" through interaction with students and academics
- collaboration with academics to address workplace problems and issues
- enhanced analytical and strategic thinking skills through clarifying thoughts and ideas for another
- greater understanding of oneself and human nature through re-evaluation of personal philosophy and professional values

Organizations benefit through

- the personal and professional development of their staff who perform the roles of mentors

- the training provided to these staff members which will allow them to enhance and develop their skills of interpersonal communication and supervisory management

- having the student as a member of the organization over a long period of time, which will allow the student to develop competencies and skills from which the organization can benefit during the internship

Information professions benefit from
- an expanded pool of highly skilled and committed professionals
- a greater role in the education of new professionals

Students benefit through
- opportunities to gain knowledge of the real world
- academic studies which address problems and issues in the workplace
- meaningful and stimulating learning experiences where theory and practice are closely integrated
- opportunities to develop and apply problem-solving strategies and critical thinking skills
- mentoring relationships with model practitioners
- learning experiences which facilitate the transition to competent practitioner
- inclusion of internship experiences as part of their curriculum vitae
- enhanced workplace skills

Academics benefit through
- collaborating with students and mentors to provide an education responsive to present and future needs
- collaborating with professional colleagues to address issues and problems of the profession and the workplace

4   What Is the Role of the Mentor in PAL?

PAL mentors are information workers who are considered by their employers to be excellent practitioners and who

- demonstrate effective communication skills, in particular the ability to provide constructive feedback in a direct, tactful, and sensitive manner
- maintain current knowledge regarding their own organization and the profession in general
- indicate a willingness to teach and the ability to function as role-models for the students
- display an interest in assisting with the development of new professionals

Mentors will be selected by organizational managers in consultation with the academic advisors.

The mentor will:

- attend a training session
- act as facilitator, teacher, observer, evaluator, and role model
- develop, in consultation with the academic advisor and student, the document, Plan of Learning Experiences, which guides the internship
- provide the student with tasks suitable for an emerging professional
- teach and supervise the student in performing unfamiliar tasks
- seek out additional learning experiences for the student as opportunities arise
- provide constructive feedback to the student concerning performance throughout the learning experiences
- introduce the student to other staff members and interdepartmental personnel helping to integrate the student into the social structure of the organization
- raise problems or potential problems with the academic advisor
- provide formal evaluation of the student in consultation with both student and academic supervisor
- evaluate the internship program

The student's learning experience will be further enhanced if the mentor:

- shows an interest in the student and develops an harmonious relationship to facilitate learning
- is a good role model
- gives the student the information needed to carry out the tasks effectively
- facilitates the student's assuming some responsibility for the tasks undertaken

5   What Are the Responsibilities of the Student?

Students are the central focus in PAL, and their learning experiences are paramount. With the guidance of the mentor and academic advisor, students are encouraged to participate in setting personal and professional learning goals and to assist in the design of learning activities that will achieve these goals.

Within this collaborative learning environment, students have certain responsibilities to

- participate in orientation sessions for PAL
- assist in the development of a Plan of Learning Experiences, in consultation with the mentor and academic supervisor
- maintain a record of the internship learning experiences including the Charting Student Progress
- take all steps necessary to aid assimilation into the organization;
- participate in the observational and experiential activities as set out in the Plan of Learning Experiences
- meet with the mentor and academic advisor for scheduled consultations, feedback, and evaluation
- attend student group seminars for each semester
- meet the schedule of time allocated for the workplace experiences
- comply with the working conditions of the internship workplace
- work within the code of ethics in the workplace
- keep an evaluative record in the PAL Journal for personal reflection on the experience

- maintain a record of attendance at the workplace
- act as an ambassador for the University
- evaluate the effectiveness of PAL
- develop a portfolio which provides evidence of learning and reflection upon goals and achievements
- self-assess personal, technical, and professional development at the conclusion of PAL

6   What Are the Responsibilities of the Academic Advisors?

Academic advisors will provide support for the student and mentor. They will encourage the establishment of a rapport between the participants through discussion about individual perceptions of the program. Through this, working relationships based on mutual understanding and respect will be established, resulting in a beneficial experience for all those involved.

The academic advisor will be available to:

- clarify various aspects of the program
- advise on the Plan of Learning Experiences
- review ongoing learning activities with students and mentors
- consult with the mentors regarding assessment of student performances and teaching procedures
- clarify participant roles and responsibilities when necessary
- anticipate potential problems and assist in solving these
- assist the mentor in role development
- encourage the student to view the mentor as a role model
- facilitate the collaborative nature of PAL
- coordinate the evaluation of the PAL internship

7   What Should the Plan of Learning Experiences Contain?

The Plan of Learning Experiences is an outline of the proposed learning activities and their associated outcomes for the student. The plan is developed by the mentor using as a reference the Charting Student Progress. The plan is designed in consultation with the academic supervisor and student and should retain some flexibility and scope for renegotiation where necessary. A draft Plan of Learning

Experiences will be devised and a final version approved by mentor, academic supervisor, and student before the internship begins. Major variations to the plan should be discussed with the academic supervisor. Although individually tailored, the plan will contain at a minimum:

- commencing and finishing dates
- an overview of the proposed work experiences, along with a brief statement about what the student should learn as a result
- schedule of consultations between mentor and student for review and evaluation
- explanation of how the student will be supervised

8   How Does PAL Fit within the Student's Course of Study?

Students who are awarded the undergraduate degree in Bachelor of Communication Information complete three years of full-time study. Students in the double degree complete their degree in four years of full-time study. Each year is divided into two semesters, so that either six or eight semesters of full-time study are required to complete these degrees or a longer period of time if studies are undertaken on a part-time basis.

The internship is offered in the student's third year of study. This enables the theoretical underpinning of course work to be practiced and synthesized in the workplace.

The internship provides two blocks of two weeks, plus an additional one day a week during two semesters. The total number of weeks in the internship is eight; however, linear time is not the sole measure here. The student's course of academic study and internship are mutually reinforcing and enriching, and enhanced professional maturity and competency is anticipated.

Students in PAL will attend two seminars in each semester to provide the opportunity to discuss and evaluate theory in the light of workplace practices and to draw together experiences of their tertiary and workplace learning environments. The students also develop a portfolio documenting their learning achievements and provide a self-assessment statement at the conclusion of PAL. These are detailed in the PAL Subject Guide.

Students gain academic credit for PAL by enrolling in the subject Partners in Learning, in semester five, with the assessment to be awarded at the conclusion of the full year.

9   What Are Some Expectations for Professional Practice?

During the PAL internship, students are expected to work within the organization's code of ethics. In addition, the following codes of professional practice are expected of the student:

- **Confidentiality and privacy**
  Information relating to personnel and the organization's internal documentation are treated as confidential unless otherwise advised by the mentor.
- **Discrimination**
  Individuals and groups will not be discriminated against for any reason including their race, class, religion, gender, age, or disability.
- **Personal conduct**
  Punctuality, reliability, and cooperativeness are expected, as are standards of dress and behavior in keeping with the organization.

10   What Are PAL's Administrative Details?

Work experiences, such as PAL, which are a formal part of a student's course of study are fully covered under the university's insurance policies which include Public Risk Liability and personal accident/injury. The details of this coverage are available on the University of Canberra Web site.

This PAL Handbook details the roles and responsibilities of students, academic staff, and mentors. The collaborative interaction built into PAL offers continuous monitoring of the progress of individual students and their mentors and the design and execution of jointly devised learning activities.

13

Charting Student Progress

Internships in Professional Education in Information Studies

Student: _____

Mentor: _____

Organization: _____

Academic Advisor: _____

This document covers the period from _____ to _____

Information Studies Program

The undergraduate information studies degree courses provide the basic education required so that the beginning professional can operate successfully in a range of information careers. As well, the program provides, through guided course planning, the opportunity to develop skills and knowledge which target specific sectors of the information professions. Each subject of study undertaken by students at the university is designed to impart professional knowledge and skills which are referred to as the "learning outcomes" of the subject. By the conclusion of their course of study, the students will have encompassed the whole of the learning outcomes.

While the basic education of the student is the responsibility of the Information Studies program, complementing academic studies with workplace experiences enhance learning and blend theory and practice to achieve a more well-rounded education than either academic studies or workplace experiences could achieve in isolation. Partners in Learning: Internships in Professional Education in Information Studies is designed to provide that well-rounded education.

Collaborative Model

PAL (Partners in Learning) is based on a collaborative teaching and learning model of opportunities for the application of theory and the practice of skills, to provide occasions for critical analysis and reflective thinking, and to facilitate personal and professional growth. Students are encouraged to set personal learning goals within the framework of their tertiary course of study and to monitor these with the assistance of the mentor and academic advisor.

The student's educational development will be viewed in a holistic manner, combining input from the student, mentor, and academic advisor over the year-long PAL internship. Each input will be considered in relation to learning outcomes applicable to the undergraduate courses as a whole. Mentors will be able to comment on the student's development using section I, Generic Outcomes, as desirable attributes applicable to a wide range of professional careers.

The learning outcomes in section II, Professional Outcomes, are expressed broadly to encompass the range of experiences and activities encompassing the students' educational preparation during their entire degree course. It is not intended that the internship would address all the learning outcomes; rather organizations should consider their individual capacity to provide learning experiences related and appropriate to these learning outcomes and the experiences and interests of the particular mentor.

It is recognized that learning experiences offered will vary from organization to organization; that the individual student's skills, knowledge, and experience will differ; and that the unique relationship between student, mentor, and academic advisor will contribute to learning outcomes in different ways. The academic course of study is designed to provide the overall framework which addresses the full range of learning outcomes.

This document which guides the evaluation of students should be viewed as assisting in their educational development. It is intended to be used to assist with planning, directing, and supervising learning activities and providing feedback on the student's progress.

As PAL is part of the student's formal course of study, the final mark will be determined by the team of academic staff in the Information Studies Program who will together review all aspects of the student's progress when determining the composite mark. The final mark will be awarded on the scale of High Distinction, Distinction, Credit, Pass, and Fail.

Feedback on the Achievement of Learning

The learning outcomes specified in the following tables are broad in scope and not intended to be mutually exclusive. The difficulty of isolating specific learning outcomes when many are clearly interrelated is recognized.

To participate in the developmental aspect of the student's performance, students and mentors will provide feedback on progress towards achieving the learning outcomes. This will be done at the end of three distinct periods of the internship: at the end of the first two-week block, at the end of first semester, and at the end of the intership.

The feedback will indicate levels of strength defined thus:

- lacks theoretical understanding and application skills
- demonstrates basic theoretical understanding and application skills
- shows emerging knowledge and skills
- performs competently and confidently
- demonstrates exemplary knowledge and skills

Feedback on the Achievement of Learning Outcomes

GENERIC OUTCOMES AND PERSONAL DEVELOPMENT (Select only the items that are relevant to the particular student's PAL experience with a tick)	After First Two Week Block						End of Semester One						End of Program					
	Opportunity to Practice Yes (Y) or No (N)	Lacks theoretical understanding & application skills	Demonstrates basic theoretical understanding & application skills	Shows emerging knowledge & skills	Performs competently & confidently	Demonstrates exemplary knowledge & skills	Opportunity to Practice Yes (Y) or No (N)	Lacks theoretical understanding & application skills	Demonstrates basic theoretical understanding & application skills	Shows emerging knowledge & skills	Performs competently & confidently	Demonstrates exemplary knowledge & skills	Opportunity to Practice Yes (Y) or No (N)	Lacks theoretical understanding & application skills	Demonstrates basic theoretical understanding & application skills	Shows emerging knowledge & skills	Performs competently & confidently	Demonstrates exemplary knowledge & skills
A. Personal Development																		
Reveals effective oral communication skills																		
Reveals effective written communication skills																		
Exercises appropriate interpersonal skills																		
Demonstrates negotiation skills																		
Displays liaison skills																		
Exhibits analytical skills																		
Shows can think critically																		
Comments																		

Feedback on the Achievement of Learning Outcomes

GENERIC OUTCOMES AND PERSONAL DEVELOPMENT (Select only the items that are relevant to the particular student's PAL experience with a tick)	After First Two Week Block						End of Semester One						End of Program					
	Opportunity to Practice Yes (Y) or No (N)	Lacks theoretical understanding & application skills	Demonstrates basic theoretical understanding & application skills	Shows emerging knowledge & skills	Performs competently & confidently	Demonstrates exemplary knowledge & skills	Opportunity to Practice Yes (Y) or No (N)	Lacks theoretical understanding & application skills	Demonstrates basic theoretical understanding & application skills	Shows emerging knowledge & skills	Performs competently & confidently	Demonstrates exemplary knowledge & skills	Opportunity to Practice Yes (Y) or No (N)	Lacks theoretical understanding & application skills	Demonstrates basic theoretical understanding & application skills	Shows emerging knowledge & skills	Performs competently & confidently	Demonstrates exemplary knowledge & skills
A. Personal Development (cont'd)																		
Demonstrates problem-solving skills																		
Shows professional commitment to what can be gained from PAL																		
Is flexible																		
Demonstrates a professional attitude																		
Takes personal responsibility for own learning outcomes																		
Shows initiative																		
Shows an increase in confidence																		
Comments																		

Feedback on the Achievement of Learning Outcomes

GENERIC OUTCOMES AND PERSONAL DEVELOPMENT (Select only the items that are relevant to the particular student's PAL experience with a tick)	After First Two Week Block						End of Semester One						End of Program					
	Opportunity to Practice Yes (Y) or No (N)	Lacks theoretical understanding & application skills	Demonstrates basic theoretical understanding & application skills	Shows emerging knowledge & skills	Performs competently & confidently	Demonstrates exemplary knowledge & skills	Opportunity to Practice Yes (Y) or No (N)	Lacks theoretical understanding & application skills	Demonstrates basic theoretical understanding & application skills	Shows emerging knowledge & skills	Performs competently & confidently	Demonstrates exemplary knowledge & skills	Opportunity to Practice Yes (Y) or No (N)	Lacks theoretical understanding & application skills	Demonstrates basic theoretical understanding & application skills	Shows emerging knowledge & skills	Performs competently & confidently	Demonstrates exemplary knowledge & skills
B. Workplace Interaction																		
Demonstrates a professional commitment to organizational needs																		
Indicates an awareness of and is sensitive to the organizational culture and is prepared to work within the culture that exists																		
Shows an understanding and knowledge of the basic functions of the workplace																		
Understands the personnel hierarchy of the staff																		
Shows an appreciation of the different areas within the organization and how they interact																		
Contributes as a team-member																		
Displays a sensitivity to interpersonal interaction																		
Comments																		

Feedback on the Achievement of Learning Outcomes

PROFESSIONAL OUTCOMES (Select only the items that are relevant to the particular student's PAL experience with a tick)	After First Two Week Block						End of Semester One						End of Program					
	Opportunity to Practice Yes (Y) or No (N)	Lacks theoretical understanding & application skills	Demonstrates basic theoretical understanding & application skills	Shows emerging knowledge & skills	Performs competently & confidently	Demonstrates exemplary knowledge & skills	Opportunity to Practice Yes (Y) or No (N)	Lacks theoretical understanding & application skills	Demonstrates basic theoretical understanding & application skills	Shows emerging knowledge & skills	Performs competently & confidently	Demonstrates exemplary knowledge & skills	Opportunity to Practice Yes (Y) or No (N)	Lacks theoretical understanding & application skills	Demonstrates basic theoretical understanding & application skills	Shows emerging knowledge & skills	Performs competently & confidently	Demonstrates exemplary knowledge & skills
A. Managing Information (as it relates to the organization)																		
Shows an understanding of who constitutes the clientele of the organization																		
Understands characteristics of online media and the systems needed to support them																		
Understands the principles of collection management																		
Comments																		

Feedback on the Achievement of Learning Outcomes

PROFESSIONAL OUTCOMES (Select only the items that are relevant to the particular student's PAL experience with a tick)	After First Two Week Block						End of Semester One						End of Program					
	Opportunity to Practice Yes (Y) or No (N)	Lacks theoretical understanding & application skills	Demonstrates basic theoretical understanding & application skills	Shows emerging knowledge & skills	Performs competently & confidently	Demonstrates exemplary knowledge & skills	Opportunity to Practice Yes (Y) or No (N)	Lacks theoretical understanding & application skills	Demonstrates basic theoretical understanding & application skills	Shows emerging knowledge & skills	Performs competently & confidently	Demonstrates exemplary knowledge & skills	Opportunity to Practice Yes (Y) or No (N)	Lacks theoretical understanding & application skills	Demonstrates basic theoretical understanding & application skills	Shows emerging knowledge & skills	Performs competently & confidently	Demonstrates exemplary knowledge & skills
B. Providing Services to Clients/Patrons/Users																		
Shows an understanding of the information needs of the clientele—and how they obtain and use information																		
Can communicate with client to determine needs																		
Can analyze client request and select appropriate sources																		
Demonstrates knowledge of appropriate sources to serve client needs																		
Indicates a competency in the use of online material																		
Comments																		

Feedback on the Achievement of Learning Outcomes

PROFESSIONAL OUTCOMES (Select only the items that are relevant to the particular student's PAL experience with a tick)	After First Two Week Block						End of Semester One						End of Program					
	Opportunity to Practice Yes (Y) or No (N)	Lacks theoretical understanding & application skills	Demonstrates basic theoretical understanding & application skills	Shows emerging knowledge & skills	Performs competently & confidently	Demonstrates exemplary knowledge & skills	Opportunity to Practice Yes (Y) or No (N)	Lacks theoretical understanding & application skills	Demonstrates basic theoretical understanding & application skills	Shows emerging knowledge & skills	Performs competently & confidently	Demonstrates exemplary knowledge & skills	Opportunity to Practice Yes (Y) or No (N)	Lacks theoretical understanding & application skills	Demonstrates basic theoretical understanding & application skills	Shows emerging knowledge & skills	Performs competently & confidently	Demonstrates exemplary knowledge & skills
C. Using Information Systems and Information Technology																		
Understands the impact of information technology—processes, products, and services																		
Understands the place of networked systems in information organization and provision																		
Analyzes and selects appropriate systems for particular purposes																		
Can use a relevant range of electronic sources																		
Indicates an awareness of up-to-date developments in the field																		
Comments																		

Feedback on the Achievement of Learning Outcomes

PROFESSIONAL OUTCOMES (Select only the items that are relevant to the particular student's PAL experience with a tick)	After First Two Week Block						End of Semester One						End of Program					
	Opportunity to Practice Yes (Y) or No (N)	Lacks theoretical understanding & application skills	Demonstrates basic theoretical understanding & application skills	Shows emerging knowledge & skills	Performs competently & confidently	Demonstrates exemplary knowledge & skills	Opportunity to Practice Yes (Y) or No (N)	Lacks theoretical understanding & application skills	Demonstrates basic theoretical understanding & application skills	Shows emerging knowledge & skills	Performs competently & confidently	Demonstrates exemplary knowledge & skills	Opportunity to Practice Yes (Y) or No (N)	Lacks theoretical understanding & application skills	Demonstrates basic theoretical understanding & application skills	Shows emerging knowledge & skills	Performs competently & confidently	Demonstrates exemplary knowledge & skills
D. Project Management																		
Demonstrates an ability to set priorities																		
Demonstrates the ability to plan ahead																		
Demonstrates ability to set and to meet deadlines																		
Demonstrates an understanding of the steps involved in managing a project																		
Shows a commitment to take a project to completion																		
Comments																		

Feedback on the Achievement of Learning Outcomes

ORGANIZATION SPECIFIC PROFESSIONAL OUTCOMES (Use space below to create professional outcomes for the organization)	After First Two Week Block						End of Semester One						End of Program					
	Opportunity to Practice Yes (Y) or No (N)	Lacks theoretical understanding & application skills	Demonstrates basic theoretical understanding & application skills	Shows emerging knowledge & skills	Performs competently & confidently	Demonstrates exemplary knowledge & skills	Opportunity to Practice Yes (Y) or No (N)	Lacks theoretical understanding & application skills	Demonstrates basic theoretical understanding & application skills	Shows emerging knowledge & skills	Performs competently & confidently	Demonstrates exemplary knowledge & skills	Opportunity to Practice Yes (Y) or No (N)	Lacks theoretical understanding & application skills	Demonstrates basic theoretical understanding & application skills	Shows emerging knowledge & skills	Performs competently & confidently	Demonstrates exemplary knowledge & skills
Comments																		

Feedback on the Achievement of Learning Outcomes

ORGANIZATION SPECIFIC PROFESSIONAL OUTCOMES (Use space below to create professional outcomes for the organization)	After First Two Week Block						End of Semester One						End of Program					
	Opportunity to Practice Yes (Y) or No (N)	Lacks theoretical understanding & application skills	Demonstrates basic theoretical understanding & application skills	Shows emerging knowledge & skills	Performs competently & confidently	Demonstrates exemplary knowledge & skills	Opportunity to Practice Yes (Y) or No (N)	Lacks theoretical understanding & application skills	Demonstrates basic theoretical understanding & application skills	Shows emerging knowledge & skills	Performs competently & confidently	Demonstrates exemplary knowledge & skills	Opportunity to Practice Yes (Y) or No (N)	Lacks theoretical understanding & application skills	Demonstrates basic theoretical understanding & application skills	Shows emerging knowledge & skills	Performs competently & confidently	Demonstrates exemplary knowledge & skills
Comments																		

14

Journal

Journal
Students Name:
Mentor:

Contact Details for Your Mentor
Name:
Organization:
Address:
Phone:
Fax:
E-mail:

PAL (Record of Attendance)—1st Semester

Two-Week Block

Date started: Date finished:

Variations (please record absences, reasons for not attending, and how the time was made up):

_____

_____

One Day Per Week

Date	Start (time)	Finish (time)	Variations

Attendance satisfactory: _____

(Mentor's signature)   (Date)

Summary and Reflections of Tasks Performed First Semester

Day _____ Date: _____

_____

_____

_____

_____

_____

_____

Day _____ Date: _____

_____

_____

_____

_____

_____

_____

References

Alderman, Belle, and Patricia Milne. "Internships for Professional Education in Library and Information Studies." *Education for Library and Information Services: Australia* 12, no. 3 (1996): 23-32.

Alderman, Belle, and Patricia Milne. "Partners in Learning— Educators, Practitioners and Students Collaborate on Work-based Learning—A Case Study." *Higher Education Research & Development* 17, no. 2 (1988): 229-38.

Alderman, Belle, Patricia Milne, assisted by Kate Gemmell. *Probabilities and Possibilities: Internships and Work Experience.* [Kit comprising a nine-minute video and eighty-page book] Canberra: Faculty of Communication, University of Canberra, 1997.

Anderson, Geoff, and David Boud. "Introducing Learning Contracts: A Flexible Way to Learn." *Innovation in Education and Training International* 33, no. 4 (1996): 221-27.

Anderson, Geoff, David Boud, and Jane Sampson. "Applications in Work-based Learning." 126-33 in *Learning Contracts: A Practical Guide,* edited by Geoff Anderson. London: Kogan Page, 1996.

Ballantyne, Roy, and Jan Packer. *Making Connections: Using Student Journals as a Teaching/Learning Aid.* Canberra: HERDSA, 1995.

Barr, Alison B., Melissa A. Walters, and Dorothy W. Hagen. "The Value of Experiential Learning in Dietetics." *Journal of the American Dietetic Association* 102, no. 10 (2002): 1458-63.

Bennis, W., and B. Nanus. *Leaders.* New York: Harper and Row, 1985.

Beveridge, Ian. "Teaching Your Students to Think Reflectively: The Case for Reflective Journals." *Teaching in Higher Education* 2, no. 1 (1997): 33-43.

Biggs, John, and Catherine Tang. "Assessment by Portfolio: Constructing Learning and Designing Teaching. Advancing International Perspectives." Paper presented at the HERDSA Annual International Conference. Adelaide, 1977.

Bihl-Hulme, Judith. "Creative Thinking in Problem-based Learning."

Bihl-Hulme, Judith. "Creative Thinking in Problem-based Learning." 177-83 in *Problem-based Learning in Education for the Professions*, edited by David Boud. Sydney: HERDSA, 1985.

Birenbaum, M., and F. Douchy. *Alternatives in Assessment of Achievement, Learning Processes and Prior Knowledge.* Boston: Kluwer Academic, 1996.

Boud, David. *Enhancing Learning Through Self Assessment.* London: Kogan Page, 1995.

Boud, David. "Experience as the Base for Learning." *Higher Education Research & Development* 19, no. 1 (1993): 33-44.

Boud, David. *Implementing Student Self-assessment.* Campbelltown, New South Wales: HERDSA, 1991.

Boud, David, and David Walker. "Making the Most of Experience." *Studies in Continuing Education* 12, no. 2 (1990): 61-80.9.

Boud, David, and Grahame Feletti. "Changing Problem-based Learning." 1-14 in *The Challenge of Problem-based Learning,* edited by David Boud and Grahame I. Feletti. London: Kogan Page, 1997.

Boud, David, and John Garrick. *Understanding Learning at Work.* London: Routledge, 1999.

Boud, David, and N. Falchikov. *Qualitative Studies of Self-assessment.* London: Kogan Page, 198

Boud, David, and Susan Knights. "Designing Courses to Promote Reflective Practice." 229-34 in *Research and Development in Higher Education*, edited by Greg Ryan, Penny Little, and Ian Dunn. Campbelltown, New South Wales: HERDSA, 1994.

Boud, David, Rosemary Keogh, and David Walker. "Promoting Reflection in Learning: A Model." 18-40 in *Reflection: Turning Experience into Learning*, edited by David Boud, Rosemary Keogh, and David Walker. London: Kogan Page, 1985a.

Boud, David, Rosemary Keogh, and David Walker. "What is Reflection in Learning?" 7-17 in *Reflection: Turning Experience into Learning*, edited by David Boud, Rosemary Keogh, and David Walker. London: Kogan Page, 1985b.

Boud, David, Ruth Cohen, and David Walker. "Introduction: Understanding Learning from Experience." 1-17 in *Using Experience for Learning,* edited by David Boud, Ruth Cohen, and David Walker. Buckingham: The Society for Research into Higher Education & Open University Press, 1993.

Caldwell, Brian J., and Earl M. A. Carter. *The Return of the Mentor: Strategies for Workplace Learning.* London: Falmer Press, 1993.

Cameron-Jones, Margot, and Paul O'Hara. "Student Perceptions of the Way that they are Supervised During Work Experience: An Instrument and Some Findings." *Assessment & Evaluation in Higher Education* 24, no. 1 (1999): 91-103.

Clawson, J. G. "Mentoring in Managerial Careers" in *Work Family and the Career,* edited by C. B. Dorr. New York: Praeger, 1980.

Clifford, Valeria. "The Development of Autonomous Learners in a University Setting." *Higher Education Research & Development* 18, no. 1 (1999): 115-28.

Cohen, Norman H. *Mentoring Adult Learners: A Guide for Educators and Trainers.* Malabar, Florida: Krieger, 1995.

Daloz, Laurent A. *Effective Teaching and Mentoring.* San Francisco: Jossey-Bass, 1986.

David, A. T., and S. Hase. *The Conditions for Fostering Cooperative Education Between Higher Education and Industry.* Canberra: AGPS, 1994.

Dochy, F., M. Segers, and D. Sluijsman. "The Use of Self-, Peer- and Co-assessment in Higher Education: A Review." *Studies in Higher Education* 24, no. 3 (1999): 331-50.

Fisher, Biddy. *Mentoring.* London: Library Association Publishing, 1994.

Gibbs, Graham. *Assessing Student Centred Courses.* Oxford: Oxford Centre for Staff Development, 1995.

Hendry, Graham D., Miriam Frommer, and Richard A. Walker. "Constructivism and Problem-based Learning." *Journal of Further and Higher Education* 29, no. 3 (1999): 359-71.

Industrial Society and the ITEM Group, The. *The Line Manager's Role in Developing Talent.* London: The Industrial Society, 1990.

Johns, C. C. "Guided Reflection." In *Reflective Practice in Nursing,* edited by S. Burns and C. Bulman. Oxford: Blackwell Scientific, 1994.

Kolb, David. *The Process of Experiential Learning.* Englewood Cliffs, New Jersey: Prentice Hall, 1984.

Kram, Kathy E. *Mentoring at Work: Developmental Relationships in Oganizational Life.* London: University Press of America, 1988.

Levinson, D. J. et al. *The Seasons of a Man's Life.* New York: Knopf, 1978.

Martin, Elaine. *The Effectiveness of Different Models of Work-based University Education.* Canberra: Department of Employment, Education, Training and Youth Affairs, 1996.

McGlinn, Jeanne M. "The Impact of Experiential Learners on Student Teachers." *The Clearing House* 76, no. 5 (2003): 143-50.

Mezirow, Jack. "How Critical Reflection Triggers Transform Learning." 1-20 in *Fostering Critical Reflection in Adulthood: A Guide to Transformative and Emancipatory Learning*, edited by Jack Mezirow and associates. San Francisco: Jossey-Bass, 1990.

Milne, Patricia, and Belle Alderman. "Partners in Learning: Internships in Professional Education in Library and Information Studies." Paper presented at the 1996 Annual Conference of the Higher Education & Research Development Society of Australasia, Perth.

Morrison, Keith. "Developing Reflective Practice in Higher Degree Students Through a Learning Journal." *Studies in Higher Education* 21, no. 3 (1996): 317-32.

Mumford, A. *Developing Directors: The Learning Process*. London: Manpower Services Commission, 1987.

Murray, Margo. *Beyond the Myths and Magic of Mentoring*. San Francisco: Jossey-Bass, 1991.

Nightingale, Peggy, Ina Te Wiata, Sue Toohey, Greg Ryan, Chris Hughes, and Doug Magin. *Assessing Learning in Universities*. Sydney: Professional Development Centre, University of New South Wales, 1997.

November, Peter. "Journals for the Journey into Deep Learning: A Framework." *Higher Education Research & Development* 15, no. 1 (1996): 115-27.

O'Rourke, Rebecca. "The Learning Journal: From Chaos to Coherence." *Assessment and Evaluation in Higher Education* 23, no. 4 (1998): 403-13.

Platzer, Hazel, Jannice Snelling, and David Blake. "Promoting Reflective Practitioners in Nursing: A review of Theoretical Models and Research into the Use of Diaries and Journals to Facilitate Reflection." *Teaching in Higher Education* 9, no. 2 (1997): 103-21.

Rickard, Wendy. "Work-based Learning in Health: Evaluating the Experience of Learners, Community Agencies and Teachers." *Teaching in Higher Education* 7, no. 1 (2002): 47-63.

Ross, Bob. "Towards a Framework for Problem-based Curricula." 28-35 in *The Challenge of Problem-based Learning*, edited by David Boud and Grahame Feletti. London: Kogan Page, 1997.

Ryan, G., S. Toohey, and C. Hughes. "The Purpose, Value and Structure of the Practicum." *Higher Education* 19, no. 3 (1996): 355-77.

Toohey, Susan. "Asessment of Students' Personal Development as Part of Preparation for Professional Work—Is it Feasible?" *Assessment and Evaluation in Higher Education* 17, no. 6 (2002): 529-38.

"Wisconsin Infuses Mentoring into Veterinary School" *DVM Newsmagazine* 35, no. 1 (2004): 28.

Woods, Donald. "Problem-Based Learning and Problem Solving." 10-42 in *Problem-based Learning in Education for the Professions,* edited by David Boud. Sydney: HERDSA, 1985.

Woodward, Helen. "Reflective Journals and Portfolios: Learning Through Assessment." *Assessment and Evaluation in Higher Education* 23, no. 4 (1998): 415-23.

Index

About the Authors

Belle Alderman (B.A., University of Georgia; MLn, Emory University; DLS, Columbia University) is professor of children's literature at the University of Canberra, in Canberra, Australia. She is the collections development manager of the Lu Rees Archives, an internationally known research collection of Australian children's books, artwork and manuscripts established in 1980.

Professor Alderman's achievements have been recognized in several spheres. In the area of teaching and scholarship in education, she was short listed in the Commonwealth government's national teaching awards for outstanding university teaching. She is a fellow of the Centre for the Enhancement of Learning, Teaching, and Scholarship at the University of Canberra, chosen for her "demonstrated excellence in teaching, leadership among colleagues and scholarship in teaching." She has been recognized for her achievements in children's literature through the national Nan Chauncy Award and Dromkeen Medal.

Professor Alderman has published widely in the field of children's literature and tertiary teaching and learning. Her ten-year involvement in work-based learning with her colleague, Patricia Milne, was Commended in the National Awards for Best Practice in Adult Education/Human Resource Development awarded by the Australian Institute of Training & Development and the Australian Association of Adult and Community Education

Patricia Milne (BA, Riverina Murray Institute of Higher Education; MA, PhD, University of Canberra) is head of the School of Information Management and Tourism at the University of Canberra. With her colleague Belle Alderman, she obtained a University Teaching Grant in 1993 that allowed them to develop the model of work-based learning described in this text.

Associate Professor Milne has published widely in the field of tertiary teaching and learning, specifically in the areas of work-based learning, online teaching and group work. She is a fellow of the Centre for the Enhancement of Learning, Teaching, and Scholarship at the University of Canberra, chosen for her "demonstrated excellence in teaching, leadership among colleagues and scholarship in teaching."

She pioneered online teaching at the University of Canberra and co-ordinates and teaches in the fully online master of knowledge management.